PROGRESSIVE DRUMMING ESSENTIALS

POLYRHYTHMS, TWISTING TIME, RHYTHM THEORY, AND MORE

By **Aaron Edgar**

Edited by **Mike Dawson**

Music engraved by **Willie Rose**

Design: **BigWig Design**

Photography by **JAG Videos and Photography**

Published by:

Modern Drummer Publications

271 Route 46 West

Suite H-212

Fairfield, NJ 07004 USA

TABLE OF CONTENTS

INTRODUCTION

Progressive Drumming Essentials is a collection of articles written for *Modern Drummer* magazine. From my very first article, "Dexterity in Odd Rhythms" (Feb. 2013), which explored all the different rhythmic variations of quintuplets, to my series titled "Progressive Drumming Essentials" and beyond. These articles represent a great deal of material I've constructed over the years for my own development, and they have been a large part of finding my voice on the drums.

The book is organized into six sections (Fundamentals, Odd Subdivisions, Rhythmic Tricks, More Odd Subdivisions, Polyrhythms, and A New Perspective on Polyrhythms). Many of the chapters have been expanded beyond their originally published versions.

I believe that learning music is a journey. You'll find greater depth of understanding when you dig deeper into the material. Once you've mastered what's on the page, modify it! Make these ideas your own, and explore your own creativity. Treating these lessons in this fashion, while striving to internalize the rhythms against a steady pulse, will ultimately free you to integrate any rhythm or concept into your playing in a natural way.

I sincerely hope you have as much fun with this material as I do!

THANKS

I want to thank my good friends at Hal Leonard and *Modern Drummer*, especially Mike Dawson and Miguel Monroy, who I have the pleasure of working with directly. Also, thanks to Jared Falk, Dave Atkinson, Scott Atkins, Thomas Barth, Karl Heinz-Menzel, Larry Davidson, Peter Maranzuk, Paul J. Hermann, Darren Schoepp, Jeff Konwalchuk, Justin Bender, Kevin Radomsky, Christian Stankee, and everyone at Drumeo, Sonor, Sabian, Evans, Vater, Protection Racket, Roland, Porter & Davies, LowBoy Beaters, Kelly SHU, S-Hoops, Cympad, Sweet Spot Clutches, Drum Dots, SledgePad, Snare Weight, 12 Gauge Microphones, Entity Workshop, 78 Customs, and VK Drums. Lastly, thanks to all of my friends, my musical cohorts, my family, and most of all my mom, Alison, for putting up with countless hours of me playing the drums. I hope that one day I have even a fraction of your patience.

▶PART 1: UNDERSTANDING ODD TIME SIGNATURES

Before we start playing sick grooves in 17/16, let's start at the beginning and define time signatures. Time signatures tell us the length of a bar, or measure. This is done with a pair of numbers. The bottom number refers to a subdivision (4 = quarter notes, 8 = 8th notes, and 16 = 16th notes), and the top number tells us how many of those notes are included in one measure.

QUARTER-NOTE METERS

The most common time signature is 4/4, where we have four quarter notes per bar. You aren't limited to playing only quarter notes, though. You can use any subdivision you want, provided that the sum of those subdivisions equals the length of four quarter notes.

Let's give some quarter-note meters a try. First up is 4/4.

Now let's get away from common time (4/4) by changing the top number from 4 to 5. This means we'll have five quarter notes per measure. We'll modify the basic 4/4 groove in Example 2 by simply repeating the last quarter note. This might feel a little strange at first. Your best bet to make it feel natural is to go slowly and count out loud. I also suggest bobbing your head on the beat, because sometimes you can feel a pattern more easily when you're moving your body along with it.

Let's make this feel a little more interesting. Instead of just repeating beat 4 on beat 5, we'll try a new pattern with snare accents on beat 2 and the "&" of 4.

I encourage you to experiment further with other quarter-note meters. Some fun listening homework would be to check out Peter Gabriel's "Solsbury Hill" followed by Primus's "Year of the Parrot." Both songs are in 7/4, but they feel completely different. "Year of the Parrot" is angular and syncopated, while "Solsbury Hill" is so natural feeling that, with just a casual listen, you might not even notice that it's in an odd time signature.

8th-Note Meters

Eighth-note meters are a little bit trickier to pull off. The first time signature we're going to try is 7/8, which is essentially a bar of 4/4 minus one 8th note. The easiest way to get started with this is to drop an 8th note from the last beat of a 4/4 groove that you already know how to play. Let's do that with Example 2.

If you haven't played in 7/8 before, it's probably going to feel a bit awkward. The first step in fixing that is to count out loud and accent beat 1. So count the 16th notes ("1-e-&-a, 2-e-&-a, 3-e-&-a, 4-e"), and replace the hi-hat on beat 1 with a crash. Try bobbing your head to the beat as well.

Once you have a handle on that, set a metronome to 8th notes and go back and forth between playing four bars of Example 2 and four bars of Example 5. Repeat that pattern until the odd-time bar feels just as natural as the 4/4 bar. All it takes is relating the challenging part (the 7/8 measure) to something you're already comfortable with (the 4/4 measure). Now let's see how it feels when we spice up the 7/8 groove a little. Try alternating between the following syncopated 7/8 groove and a syncopated 4/4 beat of your choosing.

12/8 Time

This time signature is generally felt as four groupings of three 8th notes, which feels the same as playing triplets in 4/4.

You can use that same type of feel in odd time signatures. Let's try 11/8. Example 8 is especially challenging, because we don't play constant 8th notes with the hi-hats. This broken pattern helps the groove feel unique and syncopated. Spending the time to make patterns like this feel natural will not only help you play challenging grooves, but it'll also help solidify your internal pulse so you can make more standard beats feel even better.

16th Note Meters

Here's where the lesson starts to get serious. You can consider 16th-note meters as feeling either one 16th note longer than a quarter-note meter or one 16th note shorter. For example, 17/16 is essentially a bar of 4/4 plus one 16th note, and 15/16 is the opposite; it's one 16th less than a bar of 4/4.

The first thing to do is to play constant 16ths on the snare or practice pad and count them aloud. (For the final note, say "Five.") Use singles, and notice that the sticking will reverse on the repeats. Once that's comfortable, add your metronome to the mix to tighten and refine the rhythm. As in the previous examples, go back and forth between the odd-time example and a similar pattern in 4/4.

R L R L R L R L R L R L R L R L R L R   L R L R L R L R L R L R L R L R L

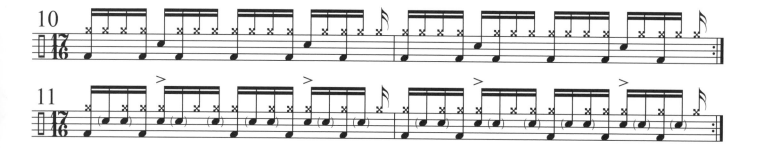

Let's try the same type of idea with 15/16. Take special notice of the bass drum pattern in Example 13.

For double bass players, Example 14 is a 21/16 groove to get you started.

In all of these examples, it's imperative that you feel beat 1 as beat 1 and not as an offbeat. Work through the patterns slowly, focus on counting out loud, and bob your head on at least beat 1 of every bar.

One of the coolest things you can do with odd time signatures is to switch them up. Patterns that consist of more than one time signature are called "composite meters." A great example of this is in Led Zeppelin's song "The Ocean," which is demonstrated in the following example.

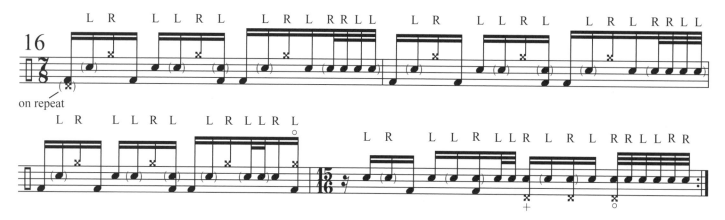

The last example is a syncopated four-bar pattern made up of three bars of 7/8 and one bar of 15/16. This groove is loosely inspired by the soundtrack music to a level in the video game *Spyro: The Dragon 3*, which was written by the great drummer Stewart Copeland. Pay special attention to the dynamics in this example. If the ghost notes are too loud, it can sound like a mess.

▶PART 2: DOUBLE BASS BOOT CAMP

One thing that can separate drummers with great double bass chops from those who struggle is their willingness to push themselves beyond their limits. You have to put in serious time if you want to get significant results. How many hours have you spent on speed and endurance? Whatever the answer, get prepared to work. If you're not exhausted after running these drills, you didn't practice hard enough.

This routine takes a little over an hour and is split into two thirty-minute sets. Each set consists of six bass drum patterns that are played for five minutes each without stopping. Even if your technique starts to fall apart, dig deep and push through until the end. The goal is to reach your breaking point and then push a little further.

Since the focus is on our feet, the hand patterns are open to interpretation. Start with the notated 8th-note hi-hat and snare pattern, but feel free to improvise as long as it doesn't interfere with your feet. A great alternative to this phrase is to match your hand pattern with the feet. (See Exercises 7–11.) Try cutting out the hands to isolate the bass drums. However, don't practice that way exclusively—fast feet are useless if you can't coordinate them with your hands.

Try practicing with tight sounds for your cymbals, because playing on washy cymbals can make it difficult to hear your bass drum accuracy. Closed hi-hats and tight stacks are my preferred choices.

Before starting with set one, stretch your legs. I like to hit all of the muscle groups from my hips down to my shins and calves. You'll be working for a while, so keep water and a towel on hand.

After stretching, strap on ankle weights and set your metronome reasonably below your maximum 32nd-note tempo. If you're not sure what that is, 70–80 bpm is a good place to start.

THE WORKOUT BEGINS

00:01–05:00: The first five minutes is a warm-up. Use this time to isolate each foot. Begin with Exercise 1, playing four bars with only the right foot and then four bars with the left foot. After a minute or two, play longer groups of 16th notes with each foot before switching.

05:01–25:00: At the five-minute mark, switch to Exercise 2 without stopping. Keep advancing continuously in five-minute increments through Exercises 3–5. Stay focused, and maintain consistency and power. If you start to cramp up, pull the notes from a different muscle group. Use your full leg (coming from your hip), your ankles, or a combination of both. Experiment with a heel-down technique to work your shin muscles. Do whatever it takes to power through.

25:01–30:00: In the last five minutes, double the amount of 32nd notes (Exercise 6). Try to push yourself close to failure. You should be barely holding on by the end. If you can make it cleanly through the entire half hour, pick a faster tempo next time.

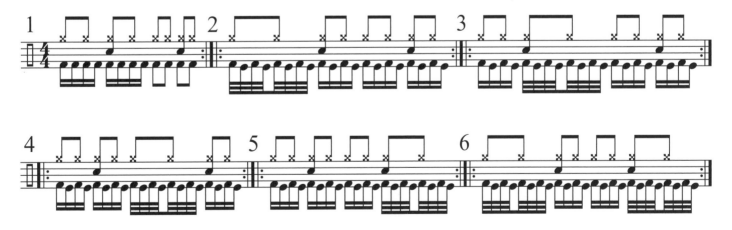

BREAK TIME

Stand up if you need to, stretch, and towel off. To keep your intensity up, don't rest too long between sets. Two or three minutes should be plenty of time. Take off your ankle weights, bump your metronome up 10 bpm, and run the entire set again.

SET TWO

30:01–55:00: You can skip the warm-up (Exercise 1), but you'll need to make up for those five minutes. Either practice one of the beats twice as long, or add one of the more advanced beats from Exercises 7–11.

55:01–60:00: At this point you should be struggling a little. Don't forget that the goal is to push yourself to your limits and beyond. If you get to the end of your second set and you still have energy, repeat the last exercise or add another full set.

The harder you push yourself, the better your results will be. If you end up going longer than an hour, try more challenging tempos or beats next time. Part of the drill here is to find your breaking point within an hour.

ADVANCED VARIATIONS

For an additional challenge, modify the intensity of the beats to suit your ability level. Exercises 7–11 each have four more 32nd notes and have been notated with the hands matching the feet on two different hi-hats.

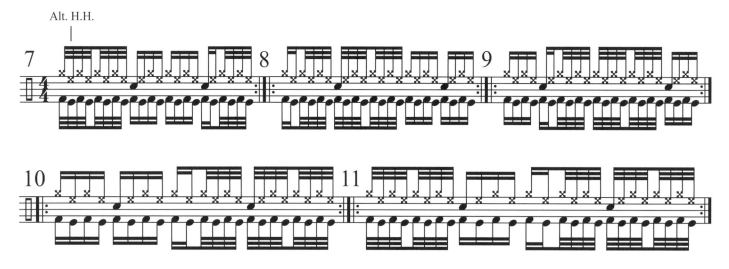

For more of a workout, try leading the entire drill with your weaker foot. If you're comfortable leading either way, try switching your lead foot every bar by adding a triplet to the end of the phrase. Exercise 12 demonstrates this idea by placing 16th-note triplets at the end of Exercise 3.

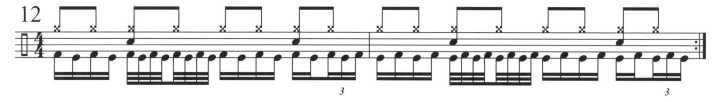

For best results, run through this set of drills two or three times per week. I wrote these exercises for my own development, and they've helped me push through some frustrating plateaus. They can do the same for you.

ADVANCED SET (60-90 MINUTES)

For those of you looking to push even further, try running two or three sets without breaks or removing the ankle weights. Do set one exactly the same, but when you get to the end, bump up the tempo without stopping and jump right into set two. You can choose to do the warm-up for five minutes, or double any of the beats within the second set. If you get to the last ten minutes and feel like you still have energy, continue into a third set with another tempo boost.

For the last ten minutes of this advanced set, try bumping up the tempo by one or two bpm every minute. The goal is to push yourself to your breaking point. If you take yourself to the edge of your abilities every time you practice, you'll have the best chance of breaking through plateaus.

►PART 3: SWITCHING GEARS

Changing subdivisions on a dime is a fundamental skill for playing double bass in modern heavy metal. Switching gears to a faster subdivision can help build intensity, and with a careful execution it sounds incredibly tight and powerful. A great example of this would be playing a 16th-note groove and then ramping up to 16th-note triplets.

BASS DRUM SUBDIVISION PYRAMID

In this example, each subdivision from 8th to 32nd notes is played on the bass drums while the hands outline a quarter-note groove. The hand pattern gives you a musical frame of reference throughout the seven subdivisions.

First focus on each example individually, and try to make it feel comfortable while playing along with a metronome. We're going to eventually put the examples together, so your starting speed will be dictated by how fast you can play a measure of 32nd notes.

RUNNING THE PYRAMID

Set your metronome a few bpm below your maximum tempo. Play the first measure for four bars, and then transition to the second measure. Focus on executing the transitions as precisely as possible - don't gradually slide into each subdivision. Practice the first two measures back and forth until they're solid. Continue with this method all the way up to 32nd notes.

When you've mastered all of the transitions, play the entire pyramid from measure 1 to 7 and back. Don't be too concerned with how many bars you spend on each subdivision. Take as much time as you need to make each of them feel comfortable. When one subdivision is settled into the pocket, make the jump to the next. If the transition is bumpy, jump back and forth until you get it tighter. Repeat this until you can switch freely between all of the subdivisions.

Another way to practice this is by matching your hands and feet. Put both hands on the hi-hat (or other tight sounds), and match the bass drum rhythm. Play an accent on the snare with whichever hand lands on beats 2 and 4. Exercise 1 demonstrates this idea in 4/4 with 16th notes and quintuplets. Practice the entire pyramid in this fashion.

ADDITIONAL GROOVE EXERCISES

Now it's time to tackle larger jumps, such as 8th-note triplets to 32nd notes. For each of these exercises, create a two-bar phrase in 4/4 comprising one bar for each subdivision. There are forty-two possibilities, however there are eight main pairs of more common transitions to master first. They are: 8th notes to 16th notes, 8th notes to 16th-note triplets, 8th notes to 32nd notes, 8th-note triplets to 16th-note triplets, 8th-note triplets to 32nd notes, 16th notes to 16th-note triplets, 16th notes to 32nd notes, and 16th-note triplets to 32nd notes.

Here's what 16th notes to 16th-note triplets looks like.

If you're feeling brave, try creating more advanced combinations, such as this quintuplet to septuplet exercise.

When you feel like you've gotten a handle on the full-measure transitions, try experimenting with shorter groupings of notes. For example, you could make a two-bar phrase in 4/4 using measures 3, 2, 3, and 5 from the pyramid.

Here are some examples that use more advanced phrasings. Exercise 6 has an odd number of notes, so the foot pattern reverses on the repeat.

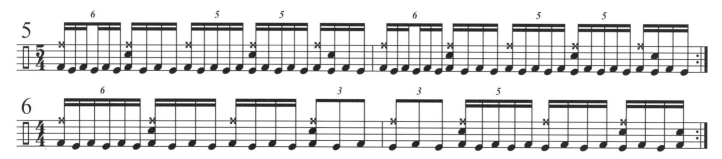

For an additional independence challenge, try different sticking patterns over alternating singles on the bass drums. Exercises 7–11 demonstrate a few alternate sticking patterns you could try for 16th notes through 32nd notes.

PARADIDDLES AND RLRRL

Paradiddle-Diddles and RLLRRLL

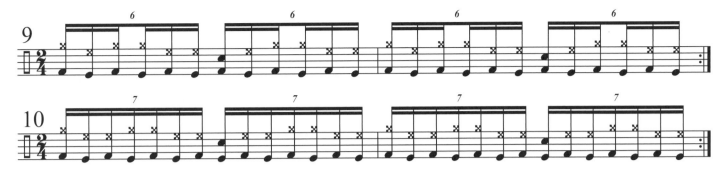

Doubles

For advanced polyrhythm junkies looking for an extra challenge, try running the pyramid while playing 8th notes on the hi-hat over each bass drum rhythm. In measures with triplets, quintuplets, and septuplets, the "&" of each beat lands on its own between bass drum notes. Go slowly, count, and good luck!

If you're having trouble placing the "and" within the quintuplet and septuplet examples, skip ahead to the polyrhythms chapter titled "Five and Seven Over Two," and come back to these exercises later.

Double Bass Subdivision Pyramid With 8ths on the Hi-Hat

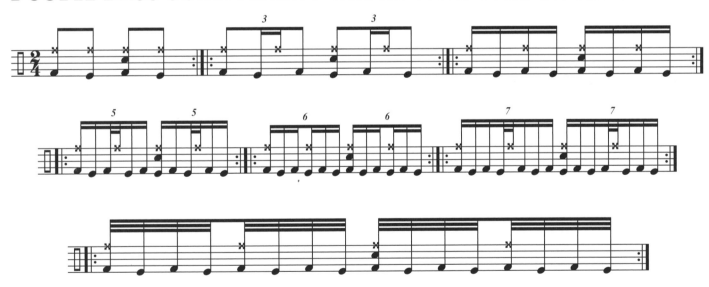

▶PART 4: SYNCOPATED DOUBLE BASS THE EASY WAY

When I began working on double bass, I was inspired by drummers like Gene Hoglan, Raymond Herrera, and Thomas Lang, all of whom seemed to have a never-ending supply of creative parts. I'd spend every waking moment figuring out their ideas and working them into my playing. From this, I stumbled on a simple concept that can be applied to even the most basic 8th-note rock grooves to turn them into heavy, syncopated double bass patterns.

We're going to use a two-step process. First, we'll take a basic 8th-note rock groove (Exercise 1) and add "e" and "a" with the left foot (Exercise 2). The bass drum notes from the basic groove will fill the spaces between the hi-hat notes, and the result will be a syncopated double bass groove, as shown in Exercise 3.

The first step toward mastering this concept is focusing on the left-foot placement. We can do this by playing the right hand on the floor tom instead of the hi-hats. You'll end up with a 16th-note roll that goes back and forth between the floor tom and bass drum. To further solidify this, try turning the pattern into a groove by placing the snare on beats 2 and 4.

In Exercise 4, the right foot plays on beat 1 and the "&" of beats 2, 3, and 4. Exercise 5 adds offbeat 16ths on the left foot. Examples 6–13 explore the concept a little bit further.

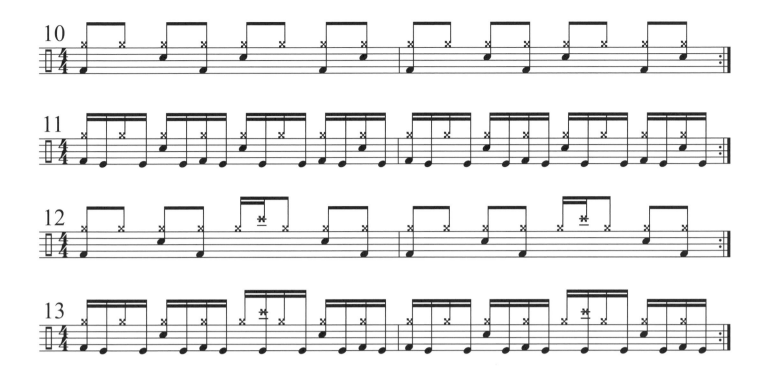

DOUBLES

In Exercise 14, there's a 32nd-note double figure with the bass drum. Be sure to phrase this strictly as 32nd notes. If you get lazy, it can start sounding like a triplet.

Exercise 15 demonstrates playing doubles with the left foot as well.

ODD-TIME EXAMPLES

Here's where things get interesting. Let's see what happens when we apply this concept to a 7/8 time signature. Be careful not to flam the snare at the end of the pattern, as it lines up with the left foot.

Exercise 17 is in a 9/8 feel. Pay special attention to your left hand, as both buzzes and ghost notes line up with the left foot. Watch your dynamics!

Next we're going to move the right-hand pattern from Exercise 17 to every third 16th note. Make sure you've got the previous exercise completely internalized before trying this. Keep in mind that the left foot is still playing consistent offbeat 16th notes. Focusing on playing the left foot smoothly can help you even out the entire pattern.

When you play an odd time signature based on 16th notes, your leading foot will switch naturally every bar. This means you'll need to learn to play offbeat notes with the right foot as well. Let's take a stab at 15/16 using this concept. You might want to isolate the second bar before trying the whole example.

For Exercise 19, I like to switch my hands, as well as my feet, every bar. If that's too challenging, you can continue leading with whichever hand is easiest in both bars. Crashing loudly on beat 1 of each bar can help you feel how the pattern repeats to solidify the transition.

Since fifteen is divisible by three, we can again replace our 8th-note hi-hat pattern with every third 16th note—except this time it will fit evenly into each bar, which will make the transition sound less choppy.

While we're diving further down the rhythmic rabbit hole, let's channel the quintuplets we spent so much time on in the last chapter and modulate Exercises 19 and 20 into quintuplets.

The next exercise places quarter notes on the hi-hat while phrasing the previous kick-and-snare pattern as quintuplets. There are a lot of empty partials here. Be sure to count ("ta, ka, din, ah, gah"), and try to play accurately. It will be helpful to program quintuplets into your metronome.

Last but certainly not least, the right hand is going to play a five-over-three polyrhythm across the previous kick-and-snare pattern.

Make sure to practice Exercises 21 and 22 into and out of more ordinary 3/4 grooves, to ensure you're able to play them in context. It's easy to lose sight of how these patterns fit musically when they're isolated.

This lesson is a prime example of how I write grooves and parts. I never take something I enjoy playing at face value, and I find it inspiring to dig deeper into the rhythms that excite me. I always say, "Modify, modify, modify." You'll usually come up with something you like just as much, if not more.

▶ PART 5: THE AMBIDEXTROUS COORDINATION CIRCUIT

This chapter is an ambidextrous study in coordination. The goal is to become comfortable playing any pattern or beat leading equally with the right and left sides of the body.

Right-handed drummers typically play with the right hand leading on a cymbal, while the left hand plays the snare and the right foot plays the bass drum. In this chapter, we're going to explore four variations of that (right-hand lead/right foot on bass drum, right-hand lead/left foot on bass drum, left-hand lead/right foot on bass drum, and left-hand lead/left foot on bass drum).

First, let's get comfortable with something relatively easy. Example 1 is a four-on-the-floor groove. Even though I'm sure you can play this with relative ease, start here to get a taste for what the beat sounds and feels like when you're playing in your comfort zone. You want to replicate this sound, dynamic balance, and feeling in the other three variations.

Start by playing the beat with your right hand on the hi-hat, right foot on the bass drum, and your left hand on the snare. Then swap your hands so that your right hand is on the snare and the left hand is playing the hi-hat. Go back and forth until those two variations sound identical and your weaker side starts to feel comfortable. Pay special attention to the dynamic balance between the limbs. The next step is to play the bass drum with your left foot under both versions.

After learning all four variations of Example 1, try adding different accent patterns on the hi-hats. Examples 2 and 3 demonstrate accenting on the downbeats and on the upbeats.

Let's try one more basic beat before we attack a more thorough method of practicing the circuit. Example 4 introduces a syncopated bass drum pattern and some ghost notes. Make sure to practice all four variations with each of the three hi-hat dynamics (no accents, accents on the downbeats, and accents on the upbeats).

Now that you have an idea of how the concept works with basic beats, let's attack smaller coordination challenges individually. Example 5 is the building blocks and demonstrates each sixteenth-note rhythm under the hi-hats.

The first step is to try playing the building blocks with just with your hands. Keep your hi-hats fairly quiet and treat each snare note as a ghost note. Once you get each pattern feeling comfortable, add in the hi-hat accent variations (no accents, downbeats, and upbeats). This material should be practiced slowly. Focus on how they sound and feel rather than how fast you can play them.

After you've gotten the hang of the building blocks, it's time to apply them to grooves. Example 6 is the framework that we'll use to explore these building blocks as ghost notes. We have a kick on beat 1, 8th notes on the hi-hats, and a snare accent on beat 3.

Next we'll apply the fifth building block from example 5 to the framework. We now have ghost notes on the first two sixteenths of each beat. Play the backbeat instead of the ghost note on beat 3.

Examples 8 and 9 demonstrate a couple more of the building blocks within the framework but with some slight embellishments.

Work your way through the rest of the building blocks in a similar fashion.

The next step is to apply the building blocks to the bass drum. Approach them the same way you did with the hands, work on them using both sides of the body, and be apply the three hi-hat accent variations. Examples 10–12 explore a few of the options.

The last example is a fun challenge in 15/16 that incorporates a variety of ghost notes from the building blocks and a bass drum pattern with five equally spaced notes across the bar. Master this leading with either hand and foot, and then work on switching your lead hand every bar and your lead foot every time you get back to the original lead hand.

SECTION 2: ODD SUBDIVISIONS

▶PART 1: DEXTERITY IN ODD RHYTHMS

In this chapter, we're going to cover how to feel quintuplets using an Indian counting system. There are many different variations, but the syllables I like to use are "ta, ka, din, ah, gah," which are easy to pronounce and can be strung together very quickly once you're comfortable with them.

Start without using a metronome and put emphasis on the first syllable, "ta," as it's landing on the quarter-note pulse. This is the most important note of the quintuplet, so if you don't have that landing solidly on the pulse, nothing you do is going to feel solid.

Now turn on your metronome and set it at a slow tempo. Don't worry about speed; precision is key. Play along with your quintuplet counting, using alternating single strokes.

Before we move on to the variations, it's important to be able to play all of the examples into and out of subdivisions that you're more comfortable with, like 16th notes. You can add the bass drum and hi-hat on quarter notes to help reinforce the pulse.

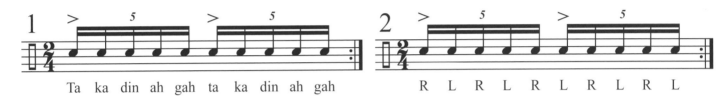

What follows is every rhythmic variation within a single quintuplet grouping. Practice these the same way as you did Example 1. Play each as an accent within the quintuplet, and keep both hands on the snare for now. Be sure to vocalize the entire quintuplet and continue to put emphasis on the first note, "ta." Add the bass drum and hi-hat underneath to help you feel the pulse.

Also be sure to practice each example into and out of a measure of 16th notes. If you work only the fives on their own, you'll have no perspective on how they relate to other subdivisions.

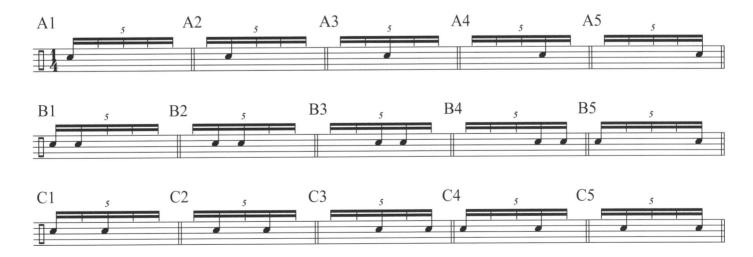

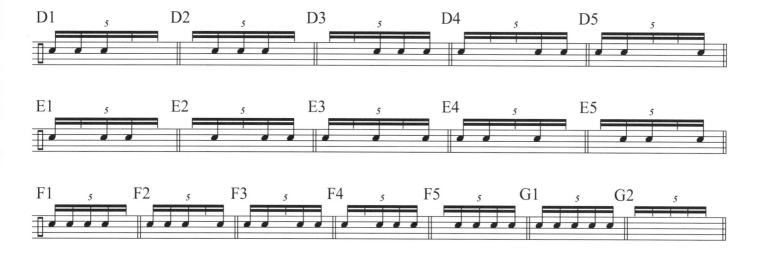

APPLYING THE RHYTHMS

The following examples demonstrate applying these quintuplet rhythms in a variety of ways. Once you've mastered playing each example on its own, try taking them in and out of a more familiar musical context, such as the beat in Example 4. Quintuplet examples A1 and B2 are applied to the toms in Examples 5 and 6.

Examples 7 and 8 apply hi-hat accents to rhythms A2 and C4.

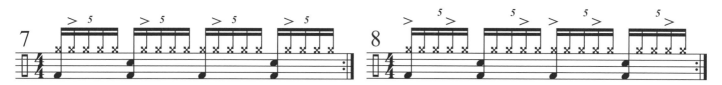

Examples 9 and 10 apply doubles to rhythms B2 and E4.

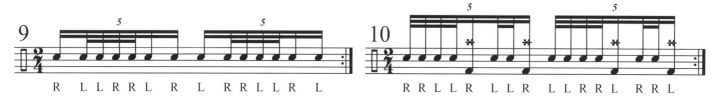

Examples 11 and 12 apply flams to rhythms A3 and B5.

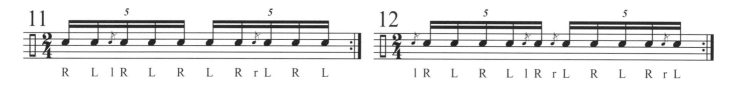

Examples 13 and 14 apply rhythms B3 and E2 as ghost notes within grooves.

Examples 15 and 16 apply rhythms A4 and F2 as bass drum notes within grooves.

Examples 17 and 18 apply rhythms E3 and D5 as hi-hat patterns.

After trying each of the application examples, pick a favorite type of phrasing and work your way through all of the quintuplet rhythm variations. Exploring the rhythms thoroughly is going to give you an incredibly strong foundation within the subdivision. Repeat this process with other phrasing applications.

    After you've explored each rhythm, start combining them. Example 19 combines rhythms C4 and C1 into a uniquely stilted hi-hat pattern. Pay special attention to the dynamics and where the hi-hat opens and closes.

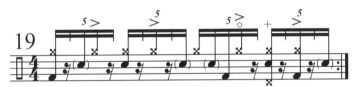

Example 20 applies rhythms C1–C5 as accents within a hi-hat pattern of alternating singles. The result is a twisted phrase that flows across the beat. The sticking pattern reverses in each bar. Take this example slowly, and exaggerate the dynamics. Unaccented notes should be played as quietly as possible, while the accents should be noticeably louder. When played with clear dynamic contract, this phrase has a hypnotic flow that sounds especially great when played between two pairs of hi-hats.

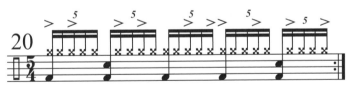

Example 21 applies C1–C5 to the the bass drum underneath a groove utilizing E3 on the hi-hat.

The last two examples explore two different ways to create a five-over-four polyrhythmic kick pattern.

▶PART 2: HOW TO FEEL ODD SUBDIVISIONS

When I was first learning quintuplets and septuplets, I would mentally cut them into smaller groups of two and three. So quintuplets would be felt as "1-2, 1-2-3" and septuplets would be felt as "1-2, 1-2, 1-2-3," with an emphasis on each 1. The problem was that it always sounded like I was feeling them that way. As much as dividing them up mentally helped me technically, it was a limitation that I wanted to break through.

The focus of this lesson is to be able to feel each subdivision without having to mentally cut it into smaller groups. Breaking away from that process will help you internalize the rhythms as entire figures so that you have much more fluid execution of them.

The first step is counting each subdivision out loud. I use an Indian counting system. There are many variations of this, but the syllables I like to use are "ta, ka, din, ah, gah" for quintuplets and "ta, ka, din, ah, ge, na, gah" for septuplets. These roll off the tongue easily and can be vocalized accurately at very high speeds. It's imperative to feel "ta" as the dominant note, as it represents the quarter-note pulse. When you're practicing, vocally accent "ta," whether or not you're accenting it on the drums.

QUINTUPLETS

The quintuplet variation example below shows each quintuplet note individually.

Let's play quintuplets as singles on the snare and accent the first note, "ta," on the toms. Pay special attention to keeping the spacing of the notes even. It's common to fudge this pattern by playing two 16th notes followed by three 16th-note triplets instead of actual quintuplets. If your metronome can sound out quintuplet and septuplet subdivisions, use that feature to help you space your notes accurately.

Playing quintuplets by themselves is a great first step, but now let's use them musically. Once you can comfortably execute Example 1, play it into and out of your favorite beats.

With rhythmic mixtures, such as in Example 2, where we go from a 16th-note groove into a quintuplet-based pattern, it's important to switch cleanly between subdivisions. Spend some time working on making the switch, just on the snare or practice pad with a metronome. The quarter notes included on the hi-hat are optional; however, they will help you form a more solid feel for the rhythms, and they're especially helpful for maintaining the pulse when switching subdivisions.

This time, instead of using the toms, let's play crashes with a bass drum hit for the second quintuplet notes, "ka." Make sure your quintuplet is solid regardless of which note you're accenting. Once you can play Example 3 by itself, go back and forth between it and different grooves, like we did in Example 2.

Examples 4–6 demonstrate the remaining quintuplet positions in the same fashion.

SEPTUPLETS

Now let's try the same ideas with septuplets.

Ta   Ka   Din   Ah   Ge   Na   Gah

In the first example below, we'll use the second septuplet note, "ka," and voice it on the toms while playing the remaining notes on the snare.

R L R L R L R L R L R L R L R L R L R L R L R L R L R L

Example 8 applies the same idea to the third note, "din."

R L R L R L R L R L R L R L R L R L R L R L R L R L R L

This time, try accenting the fourth septuplet note, "ah," with crashes and bass drum hits.

Examples 10–12 demonstrate the remaining septuplet positions on the toms.

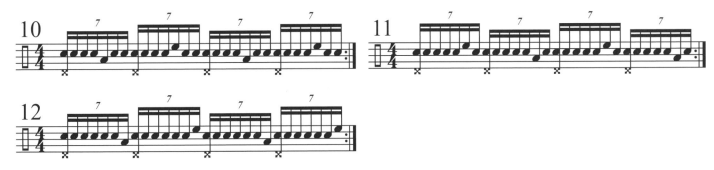

Go through the rest of the quintuplet and septuplet variations in a similar fashion. Experiment with ways to voice each note. You can use doubles, rimshots, flams...the list is limited only by your imagination. Don't forget to play the variations into and out of grooves. It's easy to lose sight of how these rhythms work musically if you don't put them into context.

DOUBLE BASS OPTIONS

Another great way to internalize any subdivision is to play it on double bass. As with the previous examples, make sure to continually switch back to a common subdivision, such as 16th notes, every two or four bars for all of the following double bass patterns.

Let's see what happens when we apply different quintuplet and septuplet spacings over double bass. Example 15 has the snare hitting on the last quintuplet while the ride outlines the quarter-note pulse.

In Example 16, the ride pattern is embellished beyond simply playing quarter notes. Pay careful attention to which foot lines up with the ride on the first, fourth, and fifth septuplet notes.

The previous examples are incredibly effective for feeling the subdivision. Hit hard, and bob your head to the quarter-note pulse. It may take many hours of practice, but eventually the patterns will feel natural.

If you want to bring polyrhythms into the fold, you can use different spacings to create some interesting and twisted patterns. Here's one that includes a five-over-six polyrhythm between the ride and snare. The snare lands on every sixth quintuplet note, which gives you five equally spaced strokes across a bar of 6/4. That's the five part of the polyrhythm. Make sure you're feeling the quarter note ride as your pulse.

You can do a similar thing by playing the septuplet spacings in a row to create a pattern with a seven-over-eight polyrhythm. This will give you seven equally spaced snare hits across two bars of 4/4. The additional ride notes introduced in Example 16 are included in Example 18 to help give the pattern a more syncopated feel.

Experiment by playing more than one accent in each subdivision. For example, play both "ta" and "ah" on the toms within a quintuplet. There are thirty-two different quintuplet rhythm variations and 128 variations of septuplets. That may seem overwhelming, but remember that every one of those is made from combinations of the note placements we've covered in this section.

▶ PART 3: INCORPORATING ODD GROUPS IN GROOVES AND FILLS

One of my favorite things to do with quintuplets and septuplets is to create syncopated, angular-sounding grooves. Exploring this unusual territory can lend itself to establishing unique feels with a lot of rhythmic tension.

In the last chapter, we discussed how to count and feel quintuplets and septuplets. To recap, I use an Indian counting system. There are many variations of this, but the syllables I like to use are "ta, ka, din, ah, gah" for quintuplets and "ta, ka, din, ah, ge, na, gah" for septuplets. When you're working on these rhythms, make sure your internal pulse stays rooted to the quarter note ("ta").

Let's take a look at a basic quintuplet fill using single strokes. It's a good idea to anchor the quarter-note pulse with your foot on the hi-hat. Go slowly and start by playing the fill one note at a time while counting out loud. Once you can play the fill comfortably, turn on the metronome and use the fill within a musical context. Try playing it with your favorite 16th-note-based groove.

Another way to use single-stroke quintuplets is to turn them into a groove. Starting with the bass drum on quarter notes, play singles between the hi-hat and snare. This naturally places the backbeats on the snare on 2 and 4. Lay into the bass drum with a solid stroke, which will help you feel the quintuplets more convincingly.

Experimenting beyond singles is a great way to start embellishing your subdivisions. Using sticking patterns that are the same length as your subdivision gives you an easy way to keep track of where you are within the odd-note grouping. A great sticking for quintuplets is RLRRL. Let's use that to create a fun fill that leads out of a 16th-note paradiddle groove.

You can use the same idea with septuplets. Here's an example of how to apply the sticking RLRLRLL to a septuplet fill. Make sure all your left-hand notes are played as subtle ghost strokes.

You don't necessarily need to play all of the notes from the subdivision. You can put rests anywhere you'd like. In Examples 5A and 5B, we're playing every other note of the quintuplet to create a five-over-two polyrhythm. Pay special attention to your quarter-note pulse, since you aren't always playing on the downbeat with the hands. Bob your head to the quarter note or play a loud bass drum stroke instead of the hi-hat if it helps you keep the time steady.

The five-over-two polyrhythm works equally well as a groove. Let's revisit Example 2 and remove the ghost notes and add some hi-hat accents. Make sure the accent pattern on the hi-hat doesn't affect your pulse. In order to get a feel for this, try playing the ghost notes (from Example 2) on your leg and hitting the accents on the snare.

Let's take a look at some sticking patterns that don't fit evenly into our subdivisions. Example 7A is an accent pattern based on the inverted paradiddle (RLLR, LRRL) spread across quintuplets on the snare. Example 7B is the same pattern orchestrated on the snare and toms. The right hand accents on the floor tom, and the left hand accents on the rack tom. Be sure to count along, which helps you form a deeper understanding of exactly where each accent goes. Dynamics are especially important here. The more you accent the toms and keep the snare quiet, the more effective this type of fill becomes. Experiment with playing bass drum/crash hits instead of the toms as well.

What's particularly cool about Examples 7A and 7B is that their accent patterns create a five-over-four polyrhythm. Let's see what happens when we try another sticking that fits unevenly into our subdivision. We'll use a three-note pattern over septuplets, orchestrated on the ride, bass drum, and snare.

Example 8 looks far more frightening than it is. The first step is to count septuplets out loud while tapping "right, left, foot." You'll need to count three full septuplets before you cycle back to having your right hand land on beat 1. Once you have a feel for the pattern away from the drumset, play it on the kit as noted below. The ride bell phrasing creates a seven-over-six polyrhythm by placing seven equally spaced notes across the six pulses of the two 3/4 measures. I used this groove on the Third Ion song "Status Undetermined" from the album *Biolith*.

While these examples may not fit into every musical situation, they're inspiring tools that can add a bit of uniqueness to your playing, and mastering them will do wonders for strengthening your internal clock. I encourage you to dig deeper into these concepts. There's a whole new world of rhythmic possibilities just waiting to be explored.

▶ PART 4: THE NOTES WE DON'T PLAY

Adding rests to complicated subdivisions can be an intimidating endeavor. But it's only tricky at first. After some diligent practice, you'll find that you've internalized an exciting new rhythmic tool.

To count quintuplets, I like to use an Indian counting system with the syllables "ta, ka, din, ah, gah." It's imperative to hear "ta" as the dominant note, as it represents the quarter-note pulse. Before jumping into Exercise 1, make sure you're comfortable counting and playing quintuplets on a practice pad.

To practice the following example, count out loud and alternate between a measure of quintuplets and the first measure of Exercise 1. In bar 1, we're only skipping three notes: "din" in beat 3, "ta" in beat 4, and "ka" in beat 5. The goal is to make the partials on either side of the rest feel as solid as they do when you're playing all five notes. Tapping quarter notes with your foot helps solidify the pulse, but be careful not to become reliant on it. After you've mastered measure 1, repeat the same process for bars 2, 3, and 4.

Once you're ready to put all four bars of Exercise 1 together, experiment with voicing the rhythms on the drumset. Start simply with a pair of surfaces, such as the snare drum and floor tom, and improvise the rhythm's orchestration between the two. Eventually expand into improvising over the entire kit. The more comfortable you are with the rhythms, the more creatively you'll be able to apply them to the drums.

When experimenting with Exercise 1, don't be afraid to modify it. You don't need to use the entire four-bar phrase; you can use pieces of it to fit into different musical contexts.

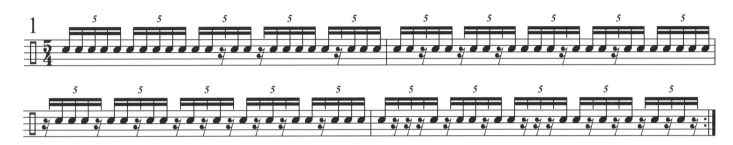

Exercises 2, 3, and 4 show some of the many ways we can apply these rhythms to the drumset. In Exercise 2, the first four quarter notes of the second measure of Exercise 1 are used as a drum fill.

Here's a groove that applies measure 4 of Exercise 1 to the hi-hats.

This next example uses the rhythm from bar 3 of Exercise 1 as a syncopated bass drum pattern in the context of a progressive-metal groove.

We'll close out the quintuplet portion of this lesson with one of my favorite grooves—the main beat I use in the song "Van Halien," the closing track on Third Ion's *13/8Bit* record. This groove uses a twenty-one-note bass drum pattern within quintuplets across four bars of 4/4. There are twenty quintuplet partials in a single bar of 4/4, which means each measure of this groove has essentially the same kick pattern displaced forward by one quintuplet partial. The pattern has six note groupings (one, two, three, two, five, and two), and each grouping is followed by a single rest. Just like we did with Exercise 1, make sure you practice slowly and count out loud. You may want to isolate the bass drum rhythm on a practice pad first.

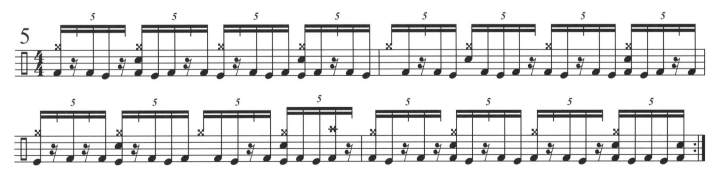

Exercises 6 and 7 incorporate rests into septuplets. Just like we did with Exercise 1, practice each of these into and out of full septuplets. Make sure you go slowly and count out loud. The syllables I like to use for counting septuplets are "ta, ka, din, ah, ge, na, gah." Again, make sure to feel "ta" as the dominant pulse.

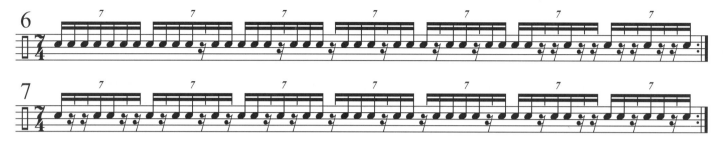

After mastering Exercises 6 and 7 on the practice pad, work on applying the rhythms to the drumset. You're only limited by your imagination. Here are some ideas to help kick-start your creativity. Exercise 8 applies the last four beats of Exercise 6 across two pairs of hi-hats in the context of a four-on-the-floor groove. Using this bass drum pattern emphasizes the quarter-note pulse. Keep practicing the example until your septuplet rhythm feels comfortable and fluid over an unwavering snare and bass drum groove.

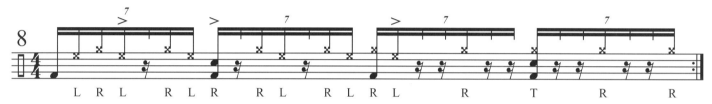

In Exercise 9, the right hand plays the first four beats of Exercise 7 while the left hand and bass drum fill in the spaces. Be mindful of your dynamics. Playing ghost strokes and unaccented notes too loudly in a busy pattern like this can end up sounding barbaric rather than tight and funky.

These rhythms are often considered odd only because we don't hear them often. But with diligent practice they won't feel strange at all. I recall the tipping point in my own progress where phrases like these started to feel so natural that I thought I was actually playing them incorrectly. Beats with odd subdivisions can feel just as good as any other groove if you allow yourself to become immersed in them.

Example 10 is the bridge section from "Van Halien." I originally wrote my part for this section by modulating every fourth and fifth quarter note into sixteenth notes and bending the kick drum pattern around that new framework. The broken sixteenths ended up making the pattern sound a little messy, so instead I filled out all of the sixteenths. The hands go back and forth between two small stacks and the snare, matching the right- and left-hand notes to the same pattern with the bass drum.

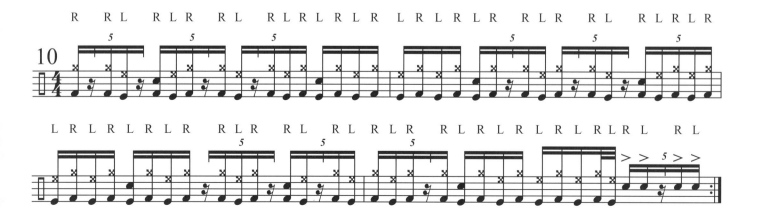

▶PART 5: A NEW REALM OF GROOVE

It might initially seem strange using the term "groove" in conversations about patterns based in odd subdivisions. But examples of these phrases being used in popular music are abundant. A perfect song to demonstrate this concept is Snoop Dogg's track "Protocol," from *More Malice*, which is clearly phrased in septuplets.

The septuplet note placement in the groove in "Protocol" creates some interesting aspects within the feel. Using this subdivision allows the final kick in each beat to be placed slightly later in the measure than if you were using 16th-note triplets. Also, the hi-hat placement falls roughly on the first three 16th notes of the beat, but the notes are slightly skewed, which creates a lazy, swung bounce with a unique twist.

To create septuplet ideas from scratch, start by replicating the rhythmic structure of more ordinary grooves. We'll use a simple set of rules to assign a 16th-note subdivision to quintuplet partials, and we'll count them using an Indian system that assigns the syllables "ta, ka, din, ah, gah" to each of the five partials in the quintuplet. The downbeat remains the same, so the first note of each quintuplet, or "ta," will represent our quarter note. The "e" of a regular 16th-note subdivision can be represented by either the second or third quintuplet partials ("ka" and "din"). The "&" can be represented by the third and fourth quintuplet notes ("din" and "ah"). And finally, the "a" can be represented by the last two quintuplet notes ("ah" and "gah").

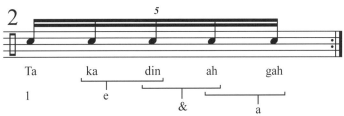

We'll start by using full quintuplets on the hi-hats to replicate the 16th-note hi-hat groove shown in Exercise 3. In Exercise 4, we change the hi-hat pattern to quintuplets and use a later placement for each of the original offbeat 16th notes—the "e" becomes the third quintuplet partial ("din"), the "&" becomes the fourth quintuplet partial ("ah"), and the "a" becomes the fifth quintuplet partial ("gah"). Exercise 5 demonstrates an alternate variation with earlier bass drum and snare placements.

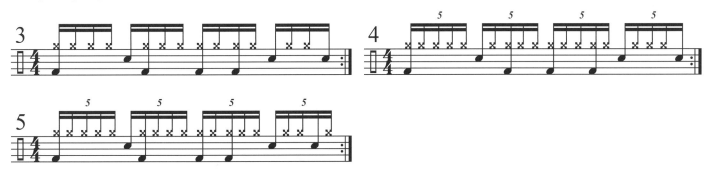

In Exercise 6, the bass drum falls on every third 16th note. To replicate this feel in quintuplets, we'll play every fourth note on the bass drum until beat 4, as noted in Exercise 7.

In Exercises 8 and 9, we have a three-note pattern—a bass drum note followed by two hi-hat notes—that's applied within a 16th and quintuplet subdivision. Keeping a strong backbeat on beats 2 and 4 helps anchor the groove. In Exercise 8, there are four bass drum notes between beats 1 and 4, and in Exercise 9 there are five bass drum notes within the same time frame.

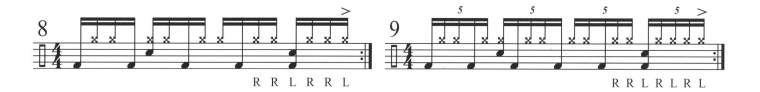

To create grooves using septuplets, we'll start with a hi-hat pattern that serves as the framework for a new groove. Exercise 10 utilizes the first, third, and sixth partial of the septuplet. Go slowly, count with the syllables "ta, ka, din, ah, ge, na, gah," and try to make the hi-hat pattern groove on its own.

Once the hi-hat pattern in Exercise 10 grooves, add the snare and bass drum.

After mastering that pattern, come up with your own kick and snare placements. I suggest keeping the backbeat on beats 2 and 4 while embellishing other parts of the phrase to ensure that it grooves.

The final two exercises interpret one of my favorite Questlove grooves from D'Angelo's "Left and Right" track off the album *Voodoo*. We'll use quintuplets and septuplets for the spacing of the hi-hat and bass drum notes. I'm not sure if Questlove was thinking this way, but you can recreate his push-and-pull feel using these subdivisions. Exercise 12 will help you internalize the feel.

The last groove in this lesson presents a few challenges. First, you have to switch subdivisions without playing all of the notes. Try counting through the subdivisions along with a metronome before moving on to the full pattern.

On beat 4 of the second measure, the hi-hat is playing straight 8th notes, with a bass drum on the last partial of a quintuplet. When counting quintuplets, the second hi-hat note lines up between "din" and "ah." Practice this slowly at first to learn how it feels.

The goal of this lesson is to prove that quintuplets and septuplets can groove. Keep an open mind, and count out loud. With diligent practice, these types of unique grooves will eventually feel natural.

SECTION 3: RHYTHMIC TRICKS

▶PART 1: BEAT DISPLACEMENT

Has a song ever caught your ear in just the right kind of wrong way, leaving the music feeling twisted? You knew the musicians were playing together correctly, and you might have even been familiar with the song, but what you felt as beat 1 was somehow wrong.

We can create this effect using beat displacement. It's primarily used as a rhythmic illusion that shifts the pulse against the rest of the music. We can also use it as a tool for writing new, interesting patterns.

Let's take an ordinary drum groove and push the beat forward by an 8th note. Our right hand will continue playing straight 8th notes on the ride cymbal, so we're only shifting the kick and snare notes forward. What was originally on beat 1 will now be on the "&" of 1.

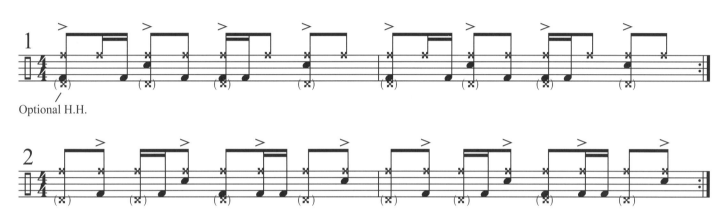

Optional H.H.

When you're working through a new displacement, it helps if you think of it as a completely new groove. You don't want to trick yourself into thinking that beat 1 is in the wrong place. To ensure we perceive this rhythm correctly, use your metronome, count out loud, and play quarter notes with your hi-hat foot.

Once you can play the two rhythms separately, try playing them for four bars each, back and forth. Play quarter notes with your hi-hat foot through both rhythms. To make the second rhythm sound convincing, you'll need to displace your dynamics as well. Try your best to stay in the pocket.

Examples 3–8 displace the pattern forward by one 8th note each time.

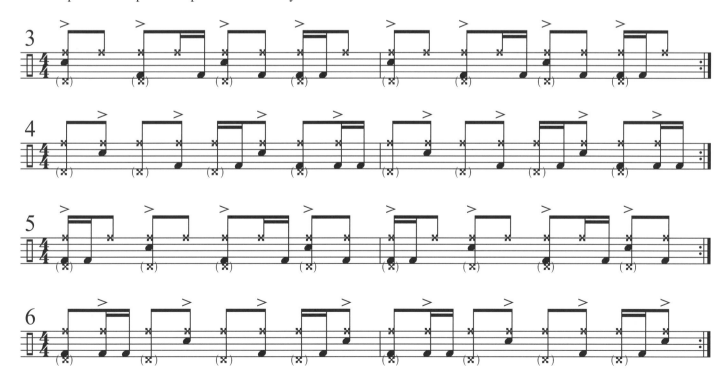

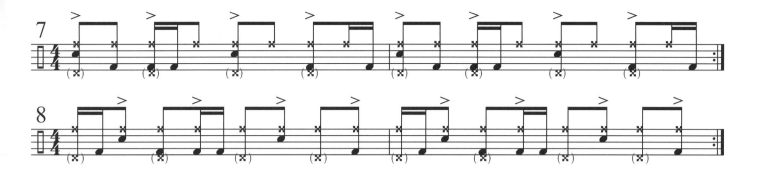

If we start on beat 1 of Exercise 8, we lose the bass drum from the beginning of the pattern. Let's see what happens if we start it on the "&" of beat 4 instead. This can be tricky to feel properly. Be sure to count out loud and play quarter notes with your hi-hat foot. Exercise 9 transitions between Exercises 1 and 8.

Once you have the hang of the previous examples individually, try running through all eight in succession by playing four bars each.

If this is the first time you've used beat displacements, spend some more time exploring the concept with your own 4/4 patterns. I find it fun to displace grooves from my favorite songs.

We can get some really interesting results when we apply displacements to less ordinary grooves. To demonstrate this, we're going to take our first rhythm, embellish it a little, and cut it into 7/8. The more out there your initial pattern is, the more your displaced beats will sound like their own unique grooves—sometimes becoming almost indiscernible from the original. This is why displacement is such a powerful writing tool, as it can yield results you wouldn't have found any other way.

Here's a more advanced groove in its basic form.

Let's try pulling beat 1 back by three 8th notes.

This is a perfect example of the displaced beat resulting in what sounds like a new groove. It's convincing enough on its own and is difficult to hear as a displacement of the original. Try playing Exercise 10 on the hi-hats for eight bars, then play Exercise 11 on the ride for eight bars. This makes a great contrast that could work beautifully as neighboring sections of a song.

Let's see how it sounds if we push the previous example forward by a quarter note. This gets especially interesting since there's no bass drum on beat 1.

Example 12 is an interesting bar of 7/8, although it may be difficult to find a place for it musically. Let's modify it into something a bit more useful. We'll add a bass drum on beat 1 and embellish the kick and snare while accenting quarter notes on a cymbal stack. The result is a really heavy, progressive groove in 7/4 with a snare drum that plays a four-over-seven polyrhythm.

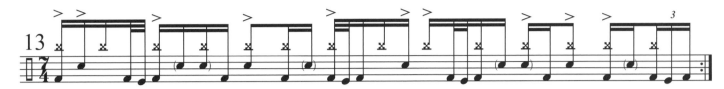

Lastly, let's talk about transitions. One of my favorite ways to transition with a displaced beat is by embellishing the groove. That way it doesn't always have to abruptly cut from one pattern to the other. Here's an example of a four-bar phrase using Exercises 1 and 3 with a brief implied shuffle for each transition.

If you want to play displacements with a band, try to get everyone to listen to the click. If your bandmates are reluctant to work with a metronome, play quarter notes with your hi-hat foot so that everyone can stay rooted to the correct pulse.

If you're looking for an additional challenge, try displacing patterns that don't have a straight 8th-note hi-hat pattern. This concept can also be applied to fills if you're looking to spice up your drumset orchestrations.

▶PART 2: ADVANCED BEAT DISPLACEMENT

To take our beat displacement prowess to a higher level, we'll learn how to shift the pulse by smaller increments. Let's focus on displacing grooves by a 16th note. A great example of this idea can be heard on the track "I'm Tweaked/Attack of the 20lb Pizza," off Vinnie Colaiuta's self-titled solo album.

Before you can start shifting the downbeat at will, you need to first learn how it feels to displace a groove to each 16th-note position against a quarter-note pulse. The most important thing to remember in these first examples is to stay rooted in the pulse. You don't want to misperceive your displacement and end up feeling beat 1 in the wrong place. Counting out loud will force you to feel the pulse correctly. Playing quarter notes with your hi-hat foot or bobbing your head to the beat also helps to feel these rhythms properly.

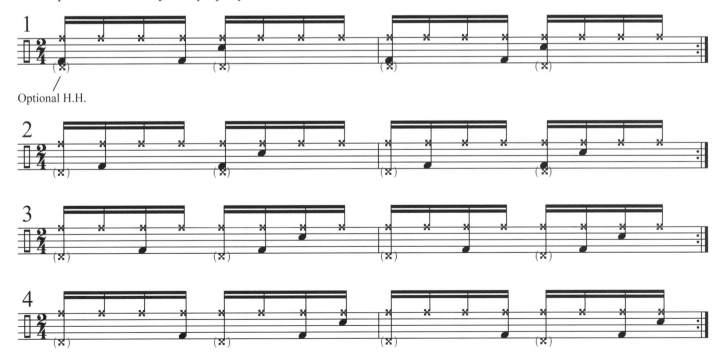

Optional H.H.

After you've mastered each displacement on its own, try playing Examples 2, 3, and 4 into and out of Example 1. Also, practice them in order. Don't forget to release the rhythmic tension you're creating with the displacements by coming back to the original pattern.

The optional quarter-note hi-hat foot notated throughout is great for learning how to feel the displacements properly and can help you when trying these ideas with other musicians. But don't become reliant on the hi-hat foot. For a more effective displacement, you might not want to highlight the pulse.

Example 5 is a warm-up exercise that can be played without a drumset by tapping your hands on your lap and your foot on the ground. Count out loud, and use your metronome. The goal is to feel the offbeat 16th notes with ease. Drill this until you can practically do it in your sleep.

The first four examples include all of the 16th notes. If you displace grooves that have 8th notes as well, you end up with some really interesting and challenging rhythms.

When learning to displace a groove with 8th notes on the ride cymbal, first displace only the kick and snare. This makes the displacement easier to internalize. It's important to spend enough time on this half-displaced groove until it feels solid and in the pocket. The deeper you can feel it, the easier it's going to be to displace your ride cymbal by a 16th note. Anchoring your left foot to quarters or 8th notes can help.

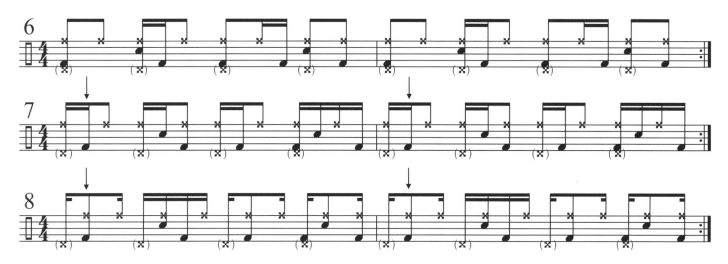

Let's try some more displacements of Example 6. In Examples 9 and 11, we'll push the pattern to start on the "a" and "e" of beat 2, respectively.

The following set of sixteen examples displaces the beat through each position of the bar. Take your time, and work out each measure individually. Begin by displacing the kick and snare, and then move your right hand only after you can feel the pattern solidly. When you have the hang of all sixteen variations, work through the entire sequence by playing two or four bars of each.

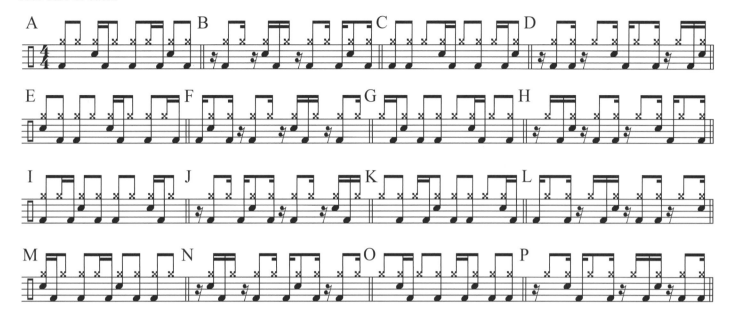

When you can comfortably play the preceding exercises, try practicing the displacements again while only looking at Example 6. In time, you'll reach a point where you can play displacements of grooves without having to write them out. You don't always need or want to start and finish displacements on beat 1, so it's important to practice beginning and ending displacements at different points in time. Let's take a new groove and see what happens if we displace it more than once in a phrase. In Example 14, we're going to restart the beat on every ninth 16th note across two bars of 4/4. The bass drum now falls on every third 16th note across the two-bar phrase.

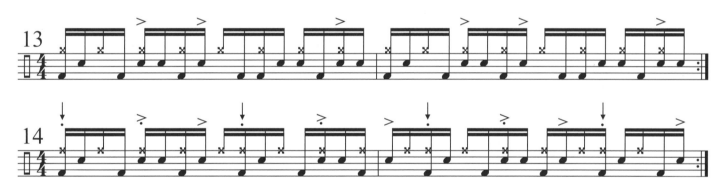

Another fun way to practice displacements is by playing a 16th-note double bass pattern while displacing your hands. I use this idea with my band Third Ion, at 2:13 in the song "Zero Mass." I keep 16th notes going on double bass and push the groove played with the hands forward each bar by a 16th note.

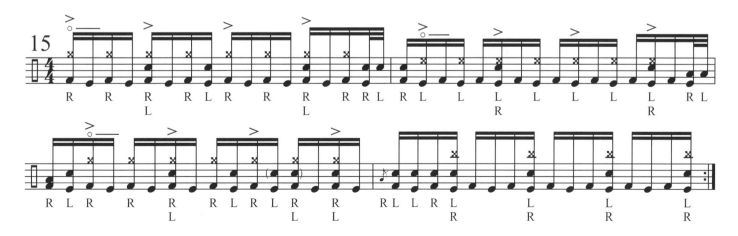

▶ PART 3: IMPLIED METRIC MODULATION MADNESS

One of my favorite rhythmic tools is implied metric modulation. This trick can make music appear to change tempos dramatically. The modulation is implied because the tempo doesn't actually change. The bpm will stay the same, but the pattern will feel faster or slower by changing its subdivision.

   People commonly hear music with a bass drum on beat 1 and backbeat on beats 2 and 4. Using different subdivisions, we can spread out the backbeat spacing to imply that time has slowed down or compress it to suggest a faster tempo. In these first examples, we're going to slow down an 8th-note rock groove by trading our 8th notes for dotted 8th notes, which are equivalent to three 16th notes.

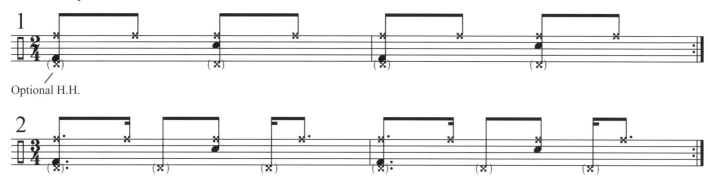

Optional H.H.

If you have trouble making Exercise 2 feel solid, try counting 16th notes out loud ("1e&a 2e&a 3e&a"), and start with the ride cymbal only. When you feel comfortable with that pattern, slowly add the bass drum and snare.

   You may have noticed that your ride cymbal in Exercise 2 creates a four-over-three polyrhythm. Metric modulation is a great tool for exploring polyrhythms, and we'll examine this application more at the end of this lesson.

   Once you get the hang of it, try playing Exercises 1 and 2 back to back for eight bars each. If you play quarter notes with your hi-hat foot, it will reinforce the original pulse and can be beneficial if you're playing these ideas with other musicians. When I'm learning new modulations, anchoring time with my left foot helps me internalize the rhythms.

   It gets interesting when we embellish this type of modulation. We can create the same effect of slowing down when modulating a 16th-note triplet groove into 16th notes.

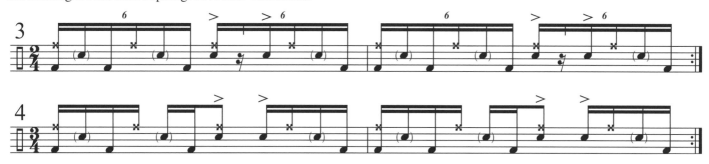

Now that we've experimented with a modulation that sounds like it's slowing down, we'll speed up an 8th-note-triplet-based shuffle groove into 16th notes.

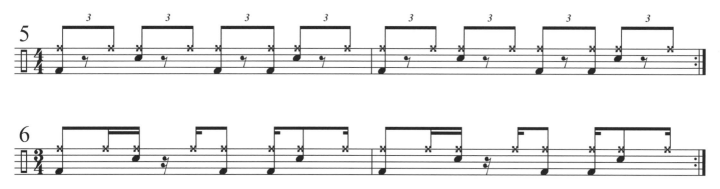

Next, try a less ordinary pattern. Exercise 7 is a funky, syncopated groove with an irregular ride pattern. Applying this phrase within 16th-note triplets yields a hypnotic two-bar phrase in 4/4.

This modulated pattern could sound like its own triplet groove. It's a perfect example of how we can use modulation as a writing tool, and we might not have come up with this using any other concept.

THE POLYRHYTHMIC CONNECTION

I mentioned earlier that you can use implied metric modulation to create grooves based on polyrhythms. In Exercises 9–11, we'll go through the process of writing an implied metric modulation groove starting with a polyrhythm.

For Exercise 9, we're going to use a four-over-five polyrhythm. We'll space four notes evenly across a bar of 5/4 time by playing every fifth 16th note. Playing quarter notes with your hi-hat foot will accentuate the polyrhythm.

The next step is to fill in the spaces with the bass drum and ghost notes. I've phrased our ride cymbal to sound like a drunken shuffle by playing the first and fourth note in each of the five 16th-note groups.

Finally, we'll modulate this groove into 4/4 using quintuplets. This gives us a backbeat on beats 2 and 4 again. Both rhythmic variations of this beat create interesting shuffle-style grooves.

Let's create another beat that starts with a polyrhythm. This time we'll explore three over four. Example 12 spaces three notes evenly across a bar of 3/4 time by playing every fourth 8th-note triplet partial. Using a two-bar phrase, you can alternate with the kick and snare to make it sound like a groove.

Just like we did with Examples 9 and 10, let's fill in some of the space to make a more interesting beat.

Let's create a more obscure-sounding seven-over-three polyrhythm by playing seven equally spaced notes on the hi-hat across a bar of 3/4. Adding alternating kick and snare notes to every second hi-hat creates a twisted version of a basic rock beat.

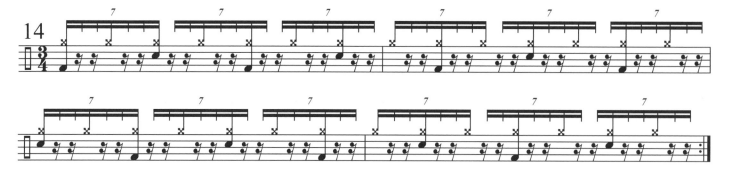

Make sure you try modulating a handful of your own grooves. Take a groove you play all the time, or transcribe a beat from one of your favorite bands and modulate it into something new. I often find that there's something inspiring hidden within a new subdivision.

Don't forget that you can also apply other rhythmic tools. Think about displacing the modulations, cutting pieces out, reversing sections, and reordering parts. You are limited only by your imagination.

▶ PART 4: MAKING FOUR SOUND LIKE MORE

I'll never forget the first time I heard the metal band Meshuggah. I was mesmerized by the amount of pocket that they were able to get from what I assumed was an odd-time signature. To my surprise, most of what they play can be written out using over-the-barline rhythms in 4/4.

"Stengah," from Meshuggah's album *Nothing*, showcases this odd phrasing technique perfectly. The opening guitar line takes up the space of eleven 8th notes and is repeated until it fills eight measures of 4/4. There are sixty-four 8th notes in eight bars of 4/4, so the 11/8 riff repeats five full times. Then the band fills the remaining 8ths with a portion of the riff before cutting back to the top on beat 1 of the ninth bar.

Example 1 contains the 11/8 "Stengah" guitar rhythm. Example 2 shows the eight-bar 4/4 drum pattern with the guitar line notated on top so you can see how the phrases interact.

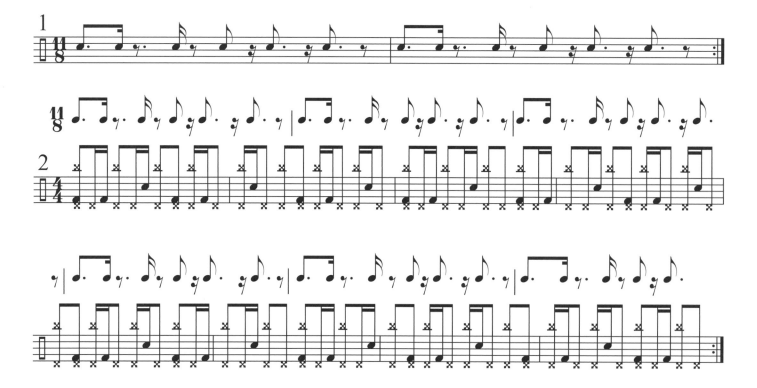

There's a lot to remember to make this eight-bar phrase work, especially since every measure differs from the one before. Pay attention to where the pattern lines up with the quarter note, which is played on the china. Every two passes of the 11/8 riff will line up on the quarter note (beat 4 of measure 3 and beat 3 of measure 6). Focusing on this can help you internalize the pattern so that you don't need to think too much about it.

Now let's focus on some shorter odd-note phrases. Example 3 has a funky bass drum figure in 5/8.

Example 4 loops the 5/8 bass drum pattern across four bars of 4/4 time, with a standard hi-hat and snare groove on top. You can think of the hand pattern as being the length of two quarter notes. With that in mind, the 5/8 bass drum rhythm lines up at the beginning of the hand pattern on beat 3 of the third measure. Playing through the 5/8 pattern twice more will leave a single quarter note at the end. You can play part of the 5/8 pattern within that space, or you can smooth over the transition with a fill.

Experiment with how the 5/8 rhythm works across different numbers of measures. For instance, try a shorter two-bar pattern. You'll have to cut off the 5/8 rhythm at the end to make it fit.

To make the rhythm resolve naturally in 4/4, add one measure to the end of Exercise 4. The result is a five-bar phrase of 4/4 in which the 5/8 rhythm loops uninterrupted.

Now try phrasing a 13/16 bass drum and floor tom pattern across four bars of 4/4. The left foot anchors the time by playing 8th notes with the hi-hat foot, and there's a backbeat on beat 3 of each bar to create a half-time feel. Adding crashes that alternate between quarter notes and the underlying rhythm creates an intense progressive metal groove.

If you're having trouble phrasing the crashes, try working through the pattern and only adding the crashes that line up on quarter notes. Gradually add in the missing crashes as you get more comfortable.

I find phrasing odd-time patterns within 4/4 compelling because it allows you to highlight the quarter-note pulse to create a stronger groove and pocket. Spend some time trying this concept with your own rhythms.

▶ PART 5: GROOVE CONTRACTION

Groove contraction can create rhythmic tension and release. Similar to how, with implied metric modulation, we can use new subdivisions to trick listeners into feeling like the quarter-note pulse has shifted, we can use the concept of contraction to make tempos feel like they've changed. Unlike metric modulation, however, groove contraction modifies the subdivision while maintaining the original quarter-note pulse.

Let's start with an 8th-note-triplet pattern between the hi-hat and snare (Exercise 1). To create tension, we'll insert another ghost note, which changes the pattern's subdivision to 16th notes (Exercise 2). Employ quiet ghost notes and consistent hi-hat accents in both phrases. Using your metronome, transition back and forth between the following two exercises.

After you've mastered each hand pattern and can transition between the two, it's time to expand them into actual grooves. To create a more dramatic effect, the bass drum and snare pattern in Exercises 3 and 4 were written to sound as similar to each other as possible.

Using these examples in a playing situation can depend on your musical setting. I like to treat the "tension" version—in this case Exercise 4—as a drum fill out of the original triplet groove. Try playing Exercise 3, and on every fourth or eighth bar, play Exercise 4 as a drum fill.

DIDDLES

Next let's apply diddles to this concept. In Exercise 5 we have a 16th-note funk groove composed of paradiddles between the hi-hat and snare. We'll create our tension using paradiddle-diddles as 16th-note triplets. Alternate between these patterns, playing two bars each. Focus on your accents and bass drum placement—they're meant to resemble each other.

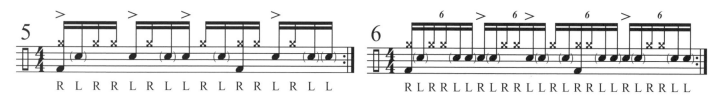

Moving the second bass drum note in Exercise 6 to the "&" of beat 3 makes these previous two grooves sound closer to one another. However, its current placement is a closer match to the bass drum and hand-pattern interaction in Exercise 5. Combining this with the faster feel of the 16th-note triplets results in an intricate and twisted version of Example 5.

Let's expand this concept further by creating similar feels within quintuplets and septuplets. We'll use a RLRRL quintuplet sticking and a RLLRRLL septuplet sticking.

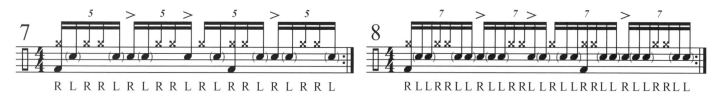

After you've worked through these grooves individually, its time to string them together. Transition through Exercises 5–8 in order of their subdivision, starting with 16th notes, then moving to quintuplets, 16th-note triplets, and finally septuplets.

The tension increases with each new subdivision as more notes are jammed in between the similar accent pattern. When you get to the end, release the tension you've created by repeating back to the start.

LINEAR PATTERNS

We can also apply contraction to linear grooves. Here we'll place less emphasis on keeping the grooves similar and instead focus on creating a longer phrase that goes through 16th-note triplets, septuplets, and 32nd notes, and then dramatically slows down with quintuplets before repeating back to 16th-note triplets. These 2/4 patterns employ a strong kick on beat 1 and an accented snare on beat 2.

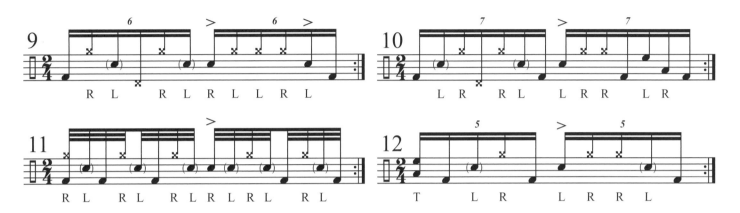

Since the quintuplets and septuplets create the most tension, let's use them as shorter transitions between the main 16th-note triplet and 32nd-note grooves. For this we'll use a pair of six-measure phrases. The first phrase consists of four bars of Exercise 9 followed by two bars of Exercise 10. Our second phrase uses five bars of Exercise 11 and one bar of Exercise 12.

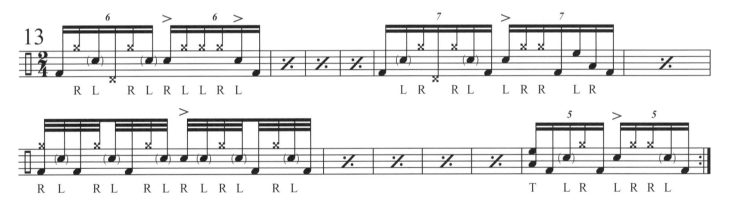

TAKING IT FURTHER

These last two examples share a pattern that's based on inverted doubles between the hi-hat and bass drum. In Exercise 14 we're playing 16th notes in 5/4, and in Exercise 15 we modulate the same pattern into 4/4 using quintuplets. Each groove has a snare backbeat on beats 2 and 4, and there's one additional snare to round out beat 5 in Exercise 14.

Exercises 14 and 15 also sound great between the bass drum and floor tom. Experiment with these patterns as well as the other grooves in this lesson. Writing your own patterns is a great method for working these concepts into your playing. You may not want to pull out this tool on every gig, but in an appropriate musical context, you can use it to create a range of subtle, powerful, and unique rhythmic statements.

SECTION 4: MORE ODD SUBDIVISIONS

▶PART 1: TORTUROUS SEPTUPLETS

I find that the best way to become proficient with a new subdivision is to isolate each partial within the grouping and then combine the partial with all of the other available notes in the subdivision. Using triplets as an example, you can play the first, second, or third note; the three different combinations of two of the notes; and all or none of the notes. This gives us a total of eight variations. When considering septuplets, however, the number of possibilities is exponentially larger, with 128 variations. We included all of them on pages 45 and 46.

Playing septuplets with double bass can set up a foundation that outlines the subdivision. This is helpful because everything you play over it will have a partial to line up with—your feet create a grid that you can use to quantize your hands.

Practicing in the context of a groove can help you internalize how septuplets feel musically. In these first exercises, we'll play septuplets with double bass in 4/4. The left hand plays a heavy quarter-note feel on a floor tom or gong drum on beat 1 and a snare backbeat on 2 and 4. When playing these exercises, count each septuplet partial out loud using the syllables "ta, ka, din, ah, ge, na, gah."

First we'll get comfortable with each individual partial. Exercise 1 places the first note of each septuplet onto a china or cymbal stack with the right hand. This reinforces our quarter-note pulse. Practice this until it feels consistent and has a solid pocket. It's important to feel this quarter-note pulse throughout all of the examples.

Exercise 2 places the china or cymbal stack on the second partial of the septuplet, or "ka." On beat 3, the right hand plays only the second septuplet note, which can be challenging. Before playing the entire groove, try looping the first half of the beat until it feels comfortable.

Examples 3 through 7 explore the remaining single-note examples.

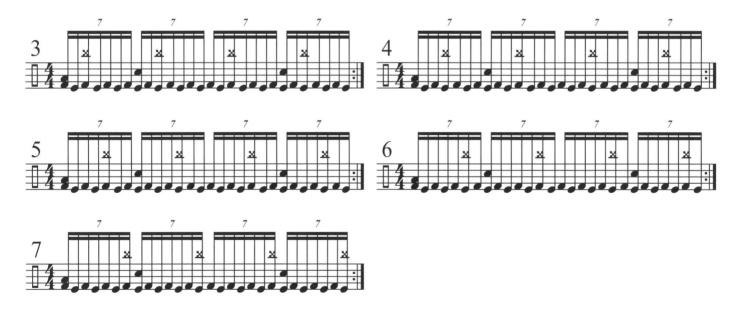

It'll take dedicated practice to be able to comfortably feel each individual note of the septuplet. But consider the previous exercises as your foundation. The 121 remaining septuplet rhythms comprise combinations of these seven notes.

Next we'll explore the two-note options. Exercise 8 adds the seventh septuplet partial to Exercise 4.

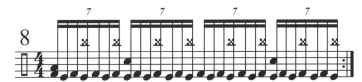

Work through all of the available possibilities in this fashion. Exercise 9 demonstrates one of the four-note variations, labeled Rhythm K6, with ghost notes added between the china or cymbal stack.

With so many rhythmic variations to work on, you can gain more benefit from your practice time if you combine other elements into these exercises. For instance, applying diddles into the septuplet bass drum pattern will force you to work on doubles with both feet.

In Exercise 10, the hands play quarter notes on the china or cymbal stack with a backbeat on the snare. There's also a double stroke in the bass drum part on the sixth partial of the septuplet (Rhythm A6).

The two-note variations are especially interesting when applying doubles to the bass drum. Exercise 11 places doubles on the second and fifth partial of each septuplet (Rhythm D2).

Once you're comfortable with the last two patterns, fill out the beat by adding a counter rhythm with a china or cymbal stack. Exercises 12 and 13 revisit the previous two examples while placing the first, third, and fifth partial of each septuplet on the china or cymbal stack (Rhythm H1).

When you start stacking multiple septuplet rhythms on top of each other, thousands of options become available. However, each variation is still a combination of the seven partials.

Exercise 14 places a ride pattern from two septuplet rhythms (Q4 and Q3) over the bass drum phrase from Exercise 9. Before trying the groove as written, get comfortable with the hand pattern over straight septuplets on double bass without the diddles. Once that's solid, add the doubles.

You can also explore septuplet variations in a polyrhythmic context by spacing the seven-note grouping over two quarter notes instead of just one. Exercise 15 lays the foundation that we'll use to continue drilling bass drum doubles. The hands play quarter notes on the china or cymbal stack with a backbeat on beats 2 and 4. The bass drum plays every second septuplet partial, which results in seven equally spaced notes over two quarter notes, or a seven-over-two polyrhythm.

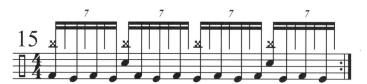

Exercises 16–22 explore playing doubles on the bass drums in each position of this new foundation.

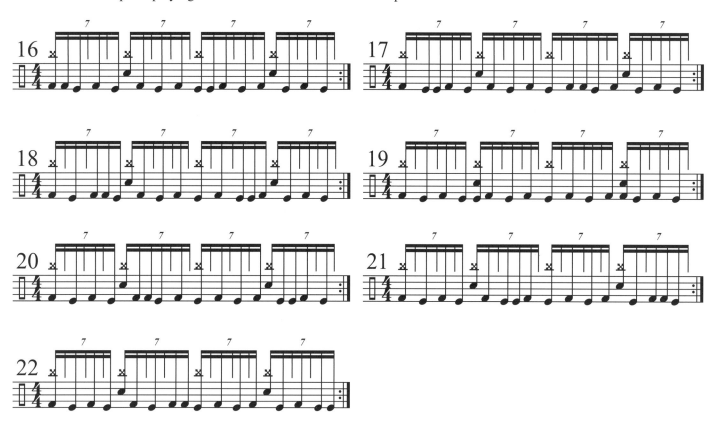

Exercise 23 explores an embellished hand pattern on the first, fourth, and fifth septuplet partial (Rhythm I1). In Exercise 24, add bass drum doubles on the third bass drum note of each seven-note grouping (Rhythm A3). In the following two exercises, unaccented snare notes should be ghosted.

At this point we've worked on balance, dynamics, time, independence, and technique, all while drilling septuplets with different rhythmic variations. Hopefully you've discovered new rhythms that inspire you. Don't be afraid to branch off and modify this concept if it speaks to you rhythmically. However, make sure to return to the original material and continue exploring.

ALL 128 SEPTUPLET RHYTHMS

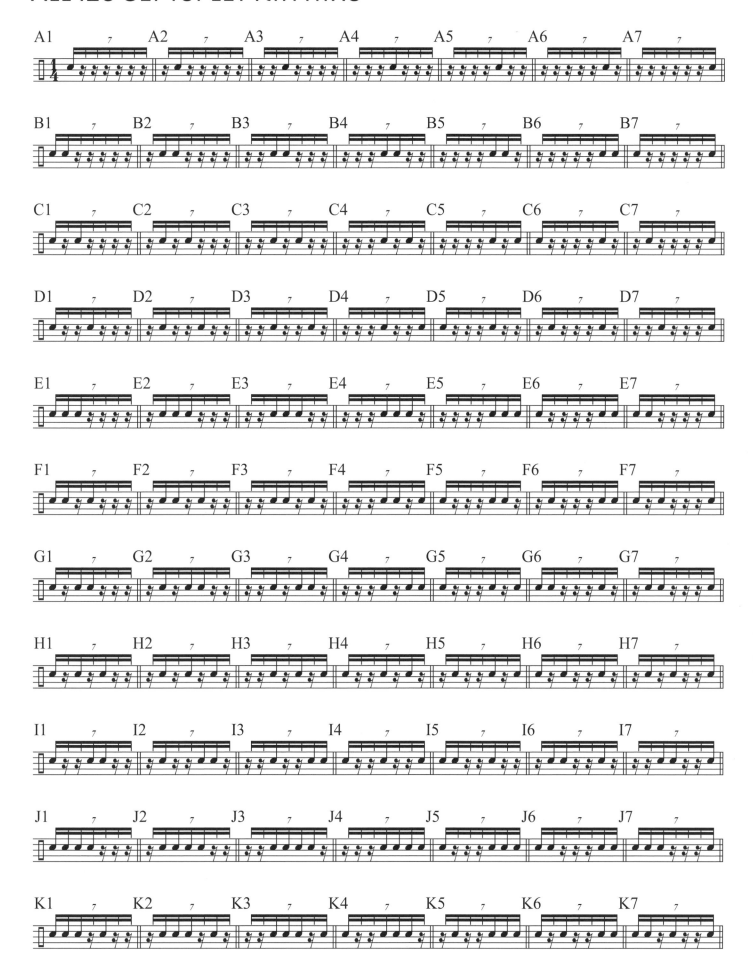

►PART 2: SEPTUPLET FIVES

Seven over five can be a challenging polyrhythm to master. We'll start building this rhythm by accenting every fifth septuplet partial in a measure of 5/4. It can take plenty of dedicated practice to master this figure, especially when we start to displace the starting position of the five-note grouping within the septuplets. However, there are some steps we can take to help internalize this rhythm.

We can lighten the load on our brain by using a sticking pattern to space out the accents. To accent every fifth note of the septuplets, we'll use a RLRRL sticking pattern and focus on the lead hand. The right hand plays one accented note followed by two unaccented ones, while the left hand plays single unaccented notes in between each right-hand group. Count the septuplets out loud using the syllables "ta, ka, din, ah, ge, na, gah," and work through the sticking pattern within the counts until it starts to feel natural. Make sure you're feeling the quarter note, or "ta," as the pulse while your hands play the syncopated rhythm on top.

When you're comfortable with Exercise 1, try playing the same pattern with your right hand on the hi-hats while your left hand plays ghost notes on the snare.

Exercise 2 places the sticking pattern into a syncopated ride cymbal groove with a slightly embellished bass drum pattern. In this and all of the exercises in this lesson, unaccented snare notes should be ghosted.

One of the biggest challenges in these exercises is internalizing the quintuplet-based accent patterns within the septuplets. Isolating smaller pieces of the phrase can help you internalize the groups of five. Exercise 3 isolates the first and second quarter notes of the previous ride pattern. Feeling rests within septuplets can be especially challenging, so be sure to take it slow and keep each partial lined up with your counting.

Once you're comfortable with Exercise 3, embellish the pattern on the bass drum and snare (Exercise 4).

One of my favorite ways to explore a new rhythm is to write out all of its permutations. Taking the five-note pattern from Exercise 3, we can create fourteen different permutations of this pattern by starting it on each piece of the beat. Exercises 5–18 demonstrate each permutation of this rhythm sequentially across two pairs of hi-hats. Pay special attention to the accents and which hand plays them. Once you've mastered the written versions, try your own orchestrations of the rhythms.

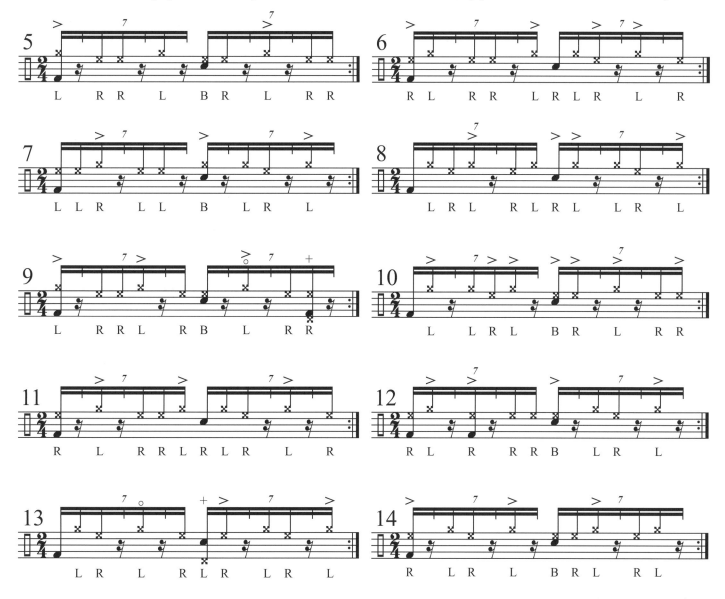

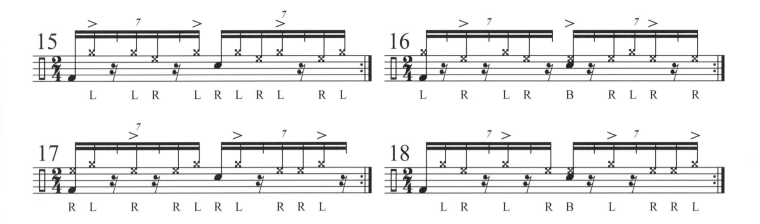

Next we'll try a different section of Exercise 2 by isolating beats 2, 3, and 4. Exercise 19 demonstrates this section of the phrase with a quarter-note bass drum pattern.

The following examples create beats using permutations of this new right-hand pattern. Focus on the syncopated kick and hi-hat accents instead of strictly accenting the quarter notes.

In Exercise 22, we'll loop another permutation of the previous pattern and place it into a bar of 4/4. Now the right-hand pattern on beat 1 occurs again on beat 4 before the whole phrase repeats.

The last example places the rhythm from Exercise 19 onto the hi-hats while replacing the right-hand hi-hat note on beat 1 with the hi-hat foot. The left foot will also play quarter notes on beats 2 and 3, which naturally opens up the hi-hats on the last partial of each septuplet.

Practicing these permutations will make the original seven-over-five polyrhythm easier to play. I also find that displacing patterns across odd rhythms almost always yields variations that I enjoy more than the original phrases. It's inspiring to know that there are new rhythms hidden within almost everything you play, if you look deep enough.

▶PART 3: ANOTHER NEW REALM OF GROOVE

Unique note placements can sometimes make a groove sound off kilter. This is fairly common in R&B and hip-hop production. But rather than quantizing or "humanizing" a pattern in recording software, which can sound random, we can create these feels by exploring unusual subdivisions.

In this section we'll explore quintuplet kick and snare placements underneath 8th-note grooves. To do this effectively, we need to perceive 8th notes and quintuplets simultaneously.

The first step is to internalize a five-over-two polyrhythm, as demonstrated in Exercise 1. In a bar of 2/4, play quarter notes on the hi-hat and every other quintuplet partial on the snare.

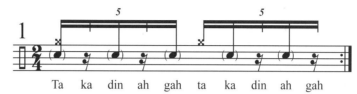

When practicing these exercises, count quintuplets out loud using the syllables "ta, ka, din, ah, gah." Make sure the snare lines up with your counting while the hi-hat holds down the pulse. Specifically on beat 2, the "ka" needs to feel like a syncopated offbeat. It can be helpful to bob your head on each "ta" to emphasize the pulse.

In Exercise 2, the rhythm is compressed into a single quarter note. Go slowly, count the quintuplet partials out loud, and try to feel the hi-hat as the pulse. The second hi-hat note falls on the "&" of the groove, which lies between the "din" and "ah" of the quintuplet. We need to feel the quintuplet partial after "&" as if it's a syncopated offbeat.

Exercise 3 sets up the framework we're going to explore in the rest of this lesson. Don't worry too much about speed here—the goal is to play a straight-8th-note pattern while counting quintuplets out loud. Being able to vocalize the quintuplet on top of the 8th-note groove will help your kick and snare placement. Spend some time immersing yourself in these initial examples before continuing.

To emphasize the pulse, try Exercise 3 with a four-on-the-floor bass drum pattern, as notated in Exercise 4.

Exercises 5–8 demonstrate the four remaining quintuplet partials within the basic groove. In Exercise 8, make sure that the bass drum lines up with the syllable "gah" (fifth quintuplet partial). It can be easy to play a lazy 16th note that resembles the quintuplet placement, but it's an entirely different exercise to count and feel this placement properly within the quintuplet.

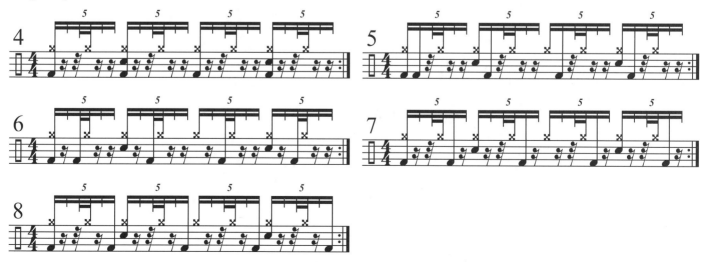

Once you're comfortable with each single-partial possibility, it's time to tackle the rest of the quintuplet rhythmic variations (located at the end of this chapter). We'll be referencing this list throughout the rest of the lesson.

The next two examples explore a couple of two-note rhythmic variations. Exercise 9 places the bass drum on the third ("din") and fifth ("gah") quintuplet partials (labeled as Rhythm C3).

Exercise 10 places the fourth ("ah") and fifth ("gah") quintuplet partials (Rhythm B4) on the bass drum, and there's an open hi-hat on beat 1. Be careful to close your hi-hat exactly on the third partial ("din") so that the right hand plays the hi-hat between the left foot and the bass drum on "ah."

The next two examples incorporate ghost notes into two-note quintuplet combinations. Exercise 11 places ghost notes on the second ("ka") and third ("din") partials (Rhythm B2), and there are some extra bass drum notes to beef up the groove.

Exercise 12 places ghost notes on the third ("din") and fifth ("gah") partials (Rhythm C3), and there's a snare buzz instead of a ghost stroke on the last note of the measure.

Exercise 13 incorporates a four-note snare, hi-hat foot, and kick figure that starts on the second quintuplet partial of each beat. An accented snare note breaks up the pattern on the last beat of the measure.

So far we've looked at rhythms that fit within one beat. The final two examples explore polyrhythmic quintuplet phrases. Exercise 14 creates a five-over-four polyrhythm by repeating a four-note bass drum pattern (every first, second, and fourth note) across a quintuplet subdivision.

The last example is in 7/4 and applies a seven-note pattern (every first, fourth, and fifth bass drum note) to the quintuplets. This creates a five-over-seven polyrhythm.

L R L

The goal is to find the pocket and groove within these patterns. It's one thing to make unique grooves by purposely playing notes slightly out of place, but that barely scratches the surface of what's possible when you start exploring a subdivision with the concepts in this lesson.

▶ PART 4: ODD SUBDIVISION OFFBEATS

When examining 32nd notes, we see that they're twice as fast as 16th notes. Similarly, we can take this idea of doubling subdivisions and apply it to any grouping. In this chapter, we're going to explore ten- and fourteen-note subdivisions, which can be viewed as the doubled equivalent of quintuplets and septuplets. When playing ten-note groupings as single strokes, your lead hand will play standard quintuplets while the opposite hand plays between them.

Exercises 1-6 outline a Johnny Rabb / Joe Morello inspired hand workout that you can use as a speed and endurance drill, and they'll also help you develop the placement of each partial in five- and ten-note groupings.

In Exercise 1, play two beats of quintuplets with your right hand followed by two beats of quintuplets with the left. Count the subdivision out loud using the syllables "ta-ka-din-ah- gah," use your metronome, and make sure all notes are even and relaxed. Exercise 1 lays the foundation for the next five examples.

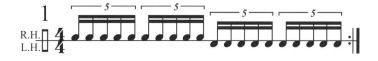

Examples 2–6 fill in all the offbeat partials of the quintuplets one at a time so that you can focus on how each note of the subdivision feels. You should still be able to feel Exercise 1 while adding the extra partials. Go slowly at first, and make sure to count out loud and focus on even and consistent spacing. Notice that the additional notes fall in between your counting.

Once you're comfortable with the previous exercises, run them in sequence. Play each one until the rhythm feels comfortable before moving on. Once you have the quintuplet version down, try the same exercises with a septuplet subdivision. Use the syllables "ta, ka, din, ah, ge, na, gah" to count septuplets.

These drills can be a lot of fun when you take them beyond the practice pad. Exercise 7 alternates the single-stroke sticking by doubling the last two partials of each ten-note grouping, and Exercise 8 applies this pattern to the drumset. The accents in these two examples outline 8th notes.

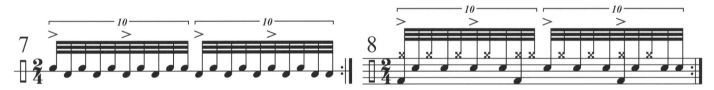

Exercise 9 utilizes septuplets to expand on Exercise 8 while incorporating a double bass pattern. Count out loud using the septuplet syllables. The counts align with the right hand on the ride cymbal during the first half of the bar and with the left hand on the hi-hat during the second half.

Exercises 10 and 11 apply short bursts of quintuplet offbeats to grooves.

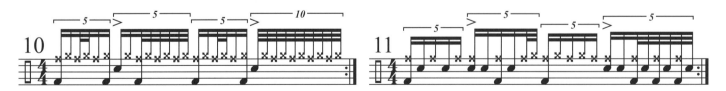

Also try using individual offbeat notes to create polyrhythmic feels. Example 12 is a quintuplet interpretation of a four-on-the-floor 16th-note hi-hat groove in which the bass drum plays 8th notes in the second half of the bar. The "&" of each beat falls in between the third and fourth quintuplet partial, or "din" and "ah."

To practice this exercise, isolate the second half of the bar with the additional bass drum notes. When you have the hang of it, play the whole measure. Focus on making the quintuplets feel consistent, and make sure your bass drum sounds solid and even underneath.

Exercise 13 places quintuplets on the bass drum and straight 8th notes on a stack or china.

Playing notes on every third partial of each ten-note grouping creates an interesting effect. In Exercise 14, we'll try this by playing a ten-over-three polyrhythm with ten equally spaced notes on the bass drum across a bar of 3/4. Our right hand plays quintuplets on the hi-hats while accenting a stack on the first and fourth partials of the quintuplet ("ta" and "ah"). The first left-hand note is meant for a floor tom or gong drum.

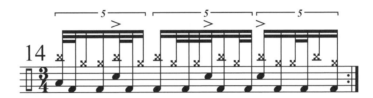

We can expand on the polyrhythmic possibilities of this idea by creating rhythms that are entirely on the offbeats. If we take a rhythm like the seven side of a seven-over-four polyrhythm and move it to the offbeats, we end up with a poly-rhythmic element that occupies a unique rhythmic space.

In Exercise 15 the first, fourth, and fifth notes of a septuplet are played with the right hand between a cymbal stack and snare. The bass drum plays septuplets while the left hand plays the seven-over-four polyrhythm starting on the first septuplet offbeat. The left-hand rhythm is notated for a floor tom or gong drum, but experiment with its placement and move it around the toms to create melodies.

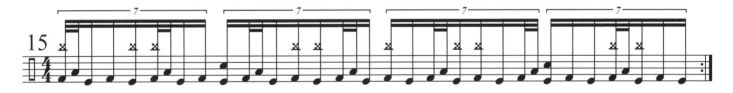

These ideas may not be the kind of rhythmic tools that you're going to pull out every single day, but they're an incredibly fun and effective way to work on your technique while also engaging your brain. If you happen to have a group of musicians willing to grit their teeth through this rhythmic storm, you'll be able to create some unique music.

▶PART 5: ADVANCED OVERLAPPING PHRASES

I've always been inspired by phrasing that seems to dance its way around the pulse. Bands such as Meshuggah apply this effect. You can bob your head in quarter notes and feel their phrases starting on different parts of the beat—sometimes for several bars—before the figure eventually lands comfortably back on beat 1. We often hear this phrasing using common subdivisions, but applying this concept to advanced subdivisions such as quintuplets or septuplets can create some incredibly unusual rhythms.

Here's a four-note pattern superimposed over quintuplets. You'll have to play the four-note phrase five times before it resolves on the first partial of the quintuplet on beat 1.

Make sure you start very slowly, somewhere around 60 bpm. Count the quintuplets out loud using the syllables "ta, ka, din, ah, gah." Go slowly, count, and practice the pattern until it feels solid.

It's imperative that you feel the bass drum as the quarter-note pulse as opposed to the hi-hat pattern. The five hi-hat accents create a five-over-four polyrhythmic feel. To really emphasize the 4/4 pulse, try adding a snare backbeat on beats 2 and 4.

The next step is to embellish the groove underneath the four-note phrase. In Exercise 2 we've added snare ghost notes and the bass drum while keeping the quarter-note pulse steady.

We can also design a groove around this phrase in which the accents follow the hi-hat pattern instead of the quarter note. Depending on how strictly you follow the pattern, you can easily create an implied metric modulation. In Exercise 3 we'll do exactly that. Don't forget that you need to feel the quarter note as your pulse, regardless of what you're playing on top of it. Don't trick yourself!

Exercise 3 can be used to transition out of Exercise 2 or for simply adding an interesting variation that creates rhythmic tension. If you play it after a similarly phrased 16th-note groove, it'll sound as if you sped up by twenty-five percent.

The next example takes a similar approach to phrasing to the one we took in Exercise 3. This time, however, we're putting emphasis on the third accented hi-hat note in each four-note grouping.

Next we're going to displace the hi-hat pattern. Don't let the notation scare you. It's the same as if you were to start Exercise 1 on beat 4 of the bar, where the first note of the hi-hat pattern starts on the second partial of the quintuplet ("ka"). To make the rhythm clearer, I've written it as a four-on-the-floor groove. When this phrase is comfortable, use it as a template to embellish some of your own beats.

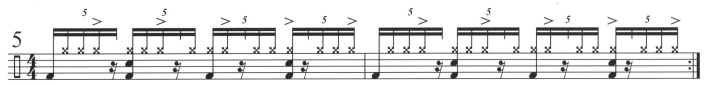

Examples 6–8 explore this new hi-hat rhythm in a few grooves.

Now let's apply some of the same steps to a five-note pattern across septuplets, which fits evenly in a bar of 5/4 time. Count out loud using the syllables "ta, ka, din, ah, ge, na, gah," and make sure you're feeling the bass drum rather than the hi-hat as the pulse.

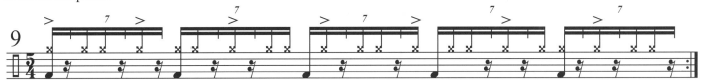

Once you have a handle on the basic version, you can embellish it into a groove. In Exercise 10, we'll continue accenting the quarter-note pulse to contrast with the hi-hat pattern. Seven equally spaced hi-hat accents in 5/4 give this groove a seven-over-five polyrhythmic feel.

In Exercise 11 we're shifting the emphasis to the five-note grouping. With the exception of beat 2, we're also accenting the quarter-note pulse. This results in a heavily syncopated groove that accents both sides of the polyrhythm. Phrasing this way is interesting because you can choose which side of the rhythm you want the rest of the band to follow. Or, for a multi-dimensional rhythmic effect, guitar and bass parts can be designed around both sides of the rhythm.

Now we'll displace the hi-hat pattern to start one note later on the second note of the septuplet ("ka"). In this exercise, the accent pattern follows the hi-hat rhythm.

So far, all of the rhythms we've explored have been shorter than the subdivisions to which they're applied. But you can implement this concept in longer phrases as well. The last rhythm we're going to try is a common eight-note pattern that could work well in 16th-note funk grooves. We'll superimpose it over septuplets and accent the first note of each eight-note phrase on a cymbal stack. This results in seven equally spaced accents over two bars of 4/4 and a seven-over-eight polyrhythmic feel.

These rhythms are often considered odd only because we don't hear them often. But they'll become much more comfortable with diligent practice. So throw on your metronome, and start exploring some unique rhythmic territory!

▶ PART 6: HERTA MY BRAIN

The herta rudiment has seen a growth in popularity recently, especially in metal. For an example, check out Tomas Haake's playing on Meshuggah's track "Bleed" off the album *Obzen*. We commonly hear this rhythm applied within 16th-note or triplet subdivisions, but hertas can create interesting ideas when applied to quintuplets and septuplets as well.

First we'll isolate hertas on each partial of a quintuplet. In Exercise 1, the herta starts on the first note of the quintuplet. Start by counting out loud and playing only the bass drum pattern until it feels comfortable. Once it's even, add the cymbal stack and snare. If you're having trouble, play quarter notes on the stack.

In Exercise 2, the herta is placed on the second quintuplet partial. In this variation, the rudiment starts with the left foot. This can be challenging, so start slowly. If you're having trouble, try reversing the footing.

Exercises 3–5 demonstrate the remaining permutations while adding an alternate stack pattern in Exercises 4 and 5. Practice all five of these examples with right- and left-foot lead.

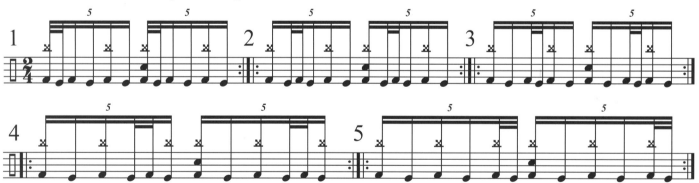

Hertas are often played consecutively, and we can phrase them this way in quintuplets as well. Try playing quarter notes on the stack until you have this next foot pattern down, and then add the embellished right hand.

Things get interesting when we play one extra partial between each herta. In the following pattern, the herta eventually falls on each quintuplet partial. The lead foot also reverses in the second measure. Try this with quarter notes on the stack before embellishing the hand pattern.

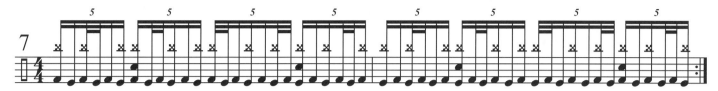

The bass drum patterns in Exercises 6 and 7 are polyrhythmic. By equally spacing five hertas over 3/4 and 4/4, we create five-over-three and five-over-four, respectively.

Here's another quintuplet example. This one is based on one of the first quintuplet herta ideas I ever wrote. The herta is applied within quintuplets on the hi-hats to create a funky, twisted 3/4 figure.

Now we'll place hertas into septuplets. Exercises 9–15 demonstrate the herta on every partial. Make sure to practice leading with either foot.

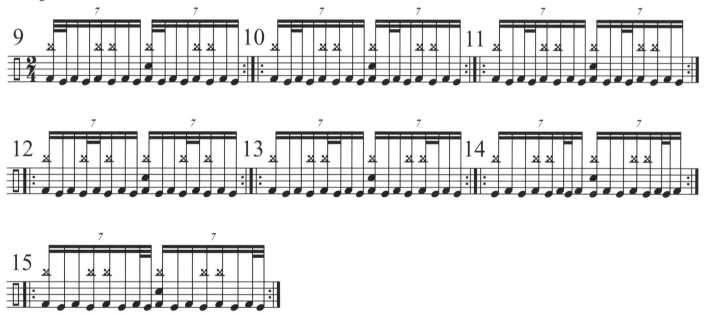

Exercise 16 places a five-note grouping into septuplets to create a seven-over-five polyrhythm with seven equally spaced hertas in a measure of 5/4. Go slowly, and count out loud while playing the bass drum pattern alone. When you can play it evenly, add the hand pattern.

We can also spread these patterns across multiple septuplets or quintuplets by adding rests. To help you learn these rhythms, program a metronome to play the full quintuplet or septuplet subdivision.

Once comfortable with Exercise 18, try splitting your feet onto different sound sources. For example, keeping your right foot on the bass drum and moving your left to the hi-hat yields an interesting variation in which your left foot plays an evenly spaced pattern on every third quintuplet partial.

We can also play hertas in odd subdivisions with the hands. In Exercise 19, our feet play solid quintuplets while the hands split hertas between the hi-hat and snare. Every third snare note is accented, but get comfortable with the basic rhythm before adding accents and ghost notes. The bass drum pattern alternates on the repeat.

Exercise 20 demonstrates an independence challenge and places the bass drum pattern from Exercise 3 underneath the hand pattern from Exercise 19. The overlapping herta phrases create a five-over-three polyrhythm. If you're having trouble, try playing straight quintuplets with the bass drum, and add in the hertas one at a time. It can be helpful to ignore the dynamics at first until you can play the pattern consistently. Then add in the ghost notes and accents.

SECTION 5: POLYRHYTHMS

▶PART 1: DEMYSTIFYING THE PROCESS

Polyrhythms, which are two contrasting subdivisions played simultaneously, can create beautifully hypnotic, entrancing patterns that dance around the pulse. They can also weave themselves into complete and utter chaos. Sometimes, when hidden subtly enough, polyrhythms enhance the music more subliminally. In recent years, bands like Meshuggah, Animals as Leaders, and Tool have played a major role in keeping these patterns popular. For progressive drummers, learning polyrhythms is a rite of passage.

When you're beginning to learn polyrhythms, you need to have a handle on independence, and your time has to be solid. You also must be ready to work your mental muscle—the brain. The best way to begin mastering polyrhythms is to break them down into their most basic form. Whether you're already a polyrhythm ninja looking to fine-tune your skills or you're simply poly-curious, working through the following steps will put you well on your way to twisting rhythms like never before.

POLYRHYTHMIC FORMULA

We're going to focus on a very precise method for determining, notating, and playing polyrhythms. At the core of this approach is what I call the polyrhythmic formula. It's a three-step process that takes the top and bottom numbers from your polyrhythm and spits out exactly what you need to know to master them.

The first polyrhythm we're going to break down is four over three.

Step 1: Take the bottom number, which in this case is three, and use that to create a quarter-note-based time signature. For four over three, this would be 3/4 time. Play quarter notes on the bass drum to outline the time signature.

Step 2: Now use the top number, which in this case is four, to determine your subdivision. Four means 16th notes. (In other polyrhythms, three will mean 8th-note triplets and two will mean 8th notes.)

Step 3: Take the bottom number again, and use it to determine the spacing you're going to use within the subdivision. For our four-over-three example, hit the snare on every third 16th note. This gives you the complete polyrhythm, with the snare outlining the four and the bass drum outlining the three.

That process can be used to break down any polyrhythm into its essential parts. To begin practicing the polyrhythm, start by hitting quarter notes with the bass drum, and play all of the 16th notes on the snare while counting out loud. Then accent every third note (1, a, &, e).

Once you have that mastered, remove the unaccented notes, leaving only the four notes of the four-over-three polyrhythm. Counting out loud might seem hard in the beginning, but you will form a deeper understanding of the rhythm, and you will internalize the polyrhythm more easily.

It's also vital that you feel the quarter note as your pulse throughout the exercises, so make sure to really put some leg into it. Don't let yourself start to feel the snare rhythm as the pulse; your rhythmic perspective is just as important as the notes themselves.

Go as slowly as necessary to count and coordinate the pattern. If you have trouble, start with only the snare part. Then add the bass drum notes one by one. Once you have the polyrhythm committed to muscle memory, turn on a metronome to help you refine and perfect the rhythm.

It's important to note that once you've internalized four over three using quarter notes, you can begin to use the polyrhythm on smaller subdivisions, such as 16ths over 8th-note triplets, which is the same rhythm, only played over a single quarter note instead of three.

Now let's see what happens when we reverse the numbers and work with the three-over-four polyrhythm.

Step 1: The bottom number is four, which gives us 4/4 time.

Step 2: The top is three, so use 8th-note triplets as your subdivision.

Step 3: Accent every fourth note of the triplet to give you three equally spaced notes over the four quarter notes.

THE EVIL TWIN

What's especially interesting about the two rhythms you just learned is that without any musical context, they sound identical. If you were to hear someone play these rhythms individually, you wouldn't be able to tell one from the other. In most cases, when you're dealing with these equal yet opposite polyrhythmic pairs, you'll find that one will be drastically more challenging to internalize than the other— that's the evil twin.

FIVE OVER FOUR

Let's use the polyrhythmic formula to break down one of the most commonly misinterpreted polyrhythms: five over four.

Step 1: The bottom number is four, which gives us 4/4 time.

Step 2: The top number is five, so our subdivision is quintuplets (five 16th notes in the space of one quarter note).

Step 3: Accent every fourth note of the quintuplets to create the five-note part of the polyrhythm.

Unless you've been playing quintuplets for a long time, the notation in Example 7 probably looks terrifying. This is the "evil twin" version. Now let's break down the opposite polyrhythm: four over five.

Step 1: The bottom number is five, which gives us 5/4 time.

Step 2: The top number is four, so we'll use 16th notes for the subdivision.

Step 3: Accent every fifth 16th note to create the four-note part of the polyrhythm.

Because it's based in the more familiar subdivision of 16th notes, four over five is drastically easier to play than five over four. But it's easy to lose your perspective with these polyrhythms, even if you're working with a metronome. To get the most out of the exercises, make sure you take each polyrhythm in and out of your favorite grooves so you learn how to apply it in a musical context.

Repeat each bar 4x

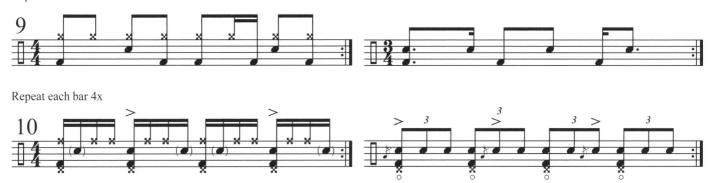

Don't forget to try the formula with other polyrhythms as well, like five over three, five over two, seven over four, and so on.

▶PART 2: GROOVE APPLICATIONS

In the last section we learned some of the theory behind polyrhythms, along with how to play these patterns in their most basic form. The next step is to learn how to use polyrhythms in grooves. Doing so will further ingrain them into your vocabulary while developing your pocket and internal pulse at the same time.

Example 1 has 16th notes on the hi-hats and four equally spaced bass drum notes in a bar of 3/4. This gives us a basic phrasing of the four-over-three polyrhythm.

It's important that you feel the quarter note as your pulse, which is outlined by the accents on the hi-hats. If you're feeling the bass drum as quarter notes, then you're actually playing a different polyrhythm: three over four (Example 2). Our rhythmic perspective is just as important as being able to play the notes correctly, if not more important.

Thinking of the bass drum as the polyrhythmic layer, add the snare on every other quarter note to imply backbeats in a 4/4 groove. You'll need to play the polyrhythm twice in order for it to resolve back to the beginning.

If we add a snare backbeat to Example 2, the result is a three-over-four polyrhythm over a four-on-the floor triplet groove, with the hi-hat supplying the polyrhythm.

Now let's embellish the last two patterns to make them a little more interesting. A combination of singles and doubles turns the three-over-four polyrhythmic groove into a super-funky, triplet-based, four-on-the-floor pattern. Dynamics are key to making this groove sound great. Focus on playing quiet ghost notes and solid, consistent accents.

This next variation uses paradiddles to embellish the hand pattern from the previous four-over-three rhythm. Using different sticking patterns is a great way to voice the numerical groupings of the polyrhythms.

RESOLUTIONS: TO FORCE OR NOT TO FORCE?

More often than not, polyrhythms won't fit evenly into a single bar of 4/4. This doesn't mean that we can't use them in 4/4; we just need to get creative. With Example 6, the first option is to simply take the first four quarter notes of the pattern and loop them (Example 7). When you do that, the polyrhythm occurs in the first three beats of the bar. The final quarter note is an incomplete piece of the rhythm. This is one of the ways we can force a polyrhythm to resolve in 4/4. It should be noted that the final quarter note doesn't need to follow the pattern, so feel free to embellish it however you'd like.

Another option is to let the rhythm resolve itself naturally in 4/4. Since the main pattern in Example 6 takes six beats to complete, playing the cycle twice takes up twelve quarter notes, which divides evenly into three bars of 4/4. That's great in theory, but music tends to be phrased in multiples of four measures. Because the groove in Example 6 takes three bars of 4/4 to resolve naturally, we can continue playing the pattern for one more bar to complete a four-bar phrase.

Another way to use polyrhythmic patterns is to treat them as groove-based fills. This can be done with a polyrhythm of any length. Just count how many beats it takes to complete the polyrhythm, and start the fill that number of beats from the end of the phrase.

Let's demonstrate this fill concept with another polyrhythm that works great in a groove setting: four over five. Example 8 is a basic phrasing of the polyrhythm, where we have four bass drum notes spaced evenly across a bar of 5/4 time.

In Example 9, we've embellished that spacing into a syncopated groove.

Since our polyrhythmic groove from Example 9 takes five quarter notes to complete, we can start it on beat 4 of the third bar of a four-bar phrase in 4/4.

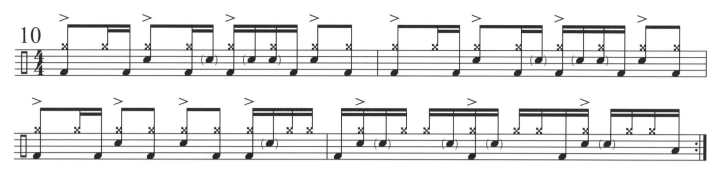

When trying to create your own polyrhythmic grooves, be sure to start with the basic phrasing and then embellish it. The polyrhythmic layer can be phrased on any instrument or combination of instruments, like the kick drum, the snare, or the hi-hat played with the foot.

It's also good practice to transcribe your own ideas to help you internalize them much faster. Seeing how various polyrhythms work in different time signatures will help you gain a much deeper understanding of them.

▶ PART 3: FIVE AND SEVEN OVER TWO

The key to internalizing any polyrhythm is to feel how the rhythm interacts with the pulse. In its most basic form, we can build a five-over-two polyrhythm by playing every other quintuplet partial over two beats. This is demonstrated in Exercise 1 with counts written below the notation. Be sure to count out loud, and play your bass drum on the "ta" of each beat. The goal is to play consistent quarter notes with your bass drum—they shouldn't feel like offbeats. Starting on beat 1, play every second quintuplet partial with your right hand while keeping an even spacing throughout the five-note grouping. "Ka" in beat 2 should feel almost like a slightly rushed offbeat 16th note.

When the rhythm is internalized, try playing a few different sticking patterns over Exercise 1. Try singles, doubles, and then paradiddles. The goal is to make the rhythm solid and consistent regardless of the sticking.

Exercise 2 demonstrates a basic version of a seven-over-two polyrhythm. Starting on beat 1, play every other septuplet partial over two beats. Use the same steps from the previous exercise to practice this example. Count out loud, and play solid quarter notes with your bass drum on the "ta" of each beat. The snare drum plays seven evenly spaced notes across the bar, and the "ka" on beat 2 should feel like an offbeat. If the second "ka" starts to feel like a downbeat, slow down and focus on counting.

Once you've internalized these rhythms, try thinking of them as quintuplets and septuplets over an 8th-note subdivision. Exercises 3 and 4 demonstrate a fun double bass application with each polyrhythm.

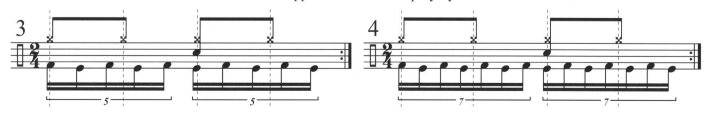

I find that the most enjoyable way to work on internalizing any polyrhythm is to apply it to a groove. If you alternate quarter notes between the bass drum and snare while layering a polyrhythm over it, you can naturally reinforce the pulse. The grooves in Exercises 5 and 6 are created from five-over-two and seven-over-two polyrhythms. Things get especially interesting when you start the polyrhythm on the subdivision's second partial, as demonstrated in Exercises 7 and 8.

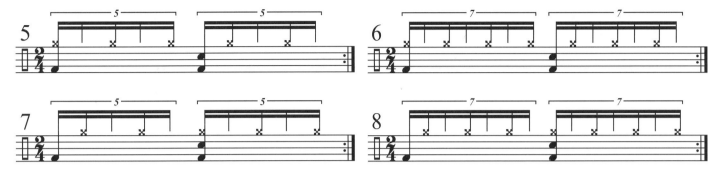

In Exercise 9, we'll start the five-over-two groove on the downbeat while filling in the spaces with ghost notes and embellishing the bass drum pattern.

Examples 10 and 11 phrase beats based on an offbeat five-over-two hi-hat pattern.

In Exercise 12, we'll play an offbeat five-over-two groove with the right hand alternating between a cymbal stack and the hi-hats, and we'll place the last note of the pattern on the floor tom. At first, try keeping your right hand on a single sound source while practicing. Add the right-hand orchestration once you've gotten the hang of the groove.

The last quintuplet example phrases a five-over-two polyrhythm on the toms. Your right hand plays ten evenly spaced notes on the floor tom while your left hand adds accents on the rack tom. Pay special attention to the hi-hat foot splashes on the "din" of each beat.

Example 14 fills in most of the spaces in a septuplet groove with seven-over-two hi-hats starting on the beat. Pay special attention to the open hi-hat on the fifth partial ("ge") in beat 4. Be sure to keep the hi-hats open through to beat 1.

(L)

Examples 15 and 16 explore offbeat seven-over-two hi-hat grooves with different accents and and openings.

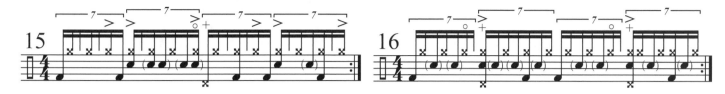

Exercise 17 demonstrates a septuplet polyrhythm groove that I call the Twisted Train. Those of you familiar with a train beat may recognize this pattern's inspiration.

A seven-over-two polyrhythm has a very unusual feel. We can use this to our advantage to build an angular variation of a 16th-note groove. In Exercise 18, we'll apply a seven-over-two polyrhythm as a contrasting rhythm to a typical 16th-note hi-hat groove. Alternate between these two feels once you've internalized the septuplet variation.

Exercise 19 embellishes a seven-over-two groove by starting the hi-hat pattern on the offbeat. Pay close attention to the rest on the beginning of beat 3. The spacing of the rest will be easier to perceive if you focus on playing straight and consistent notes with your right hand. Try to use big motions and stiffer arms when first trying this exercise; it can help keep the pattern consistent.

This last exercise combines two of the feels we've worked on into a challenging groove with some fun and nasty hi-hat openings. The first half of this beat is a seven-over-two polyrhythm that starts on the downbeat, while the second half is a five-over-two polyrhythm that begins on the offbeat. At first, try starting with either the first or second half of the beat. Count out loud with your metronome and get comfortable with the hi-hat pattern without worrying about accents yet. Once that's down, add in the rest of the beat. Lastly, add the hi-hat accents and openings. Pay special attention to the hi-hat closing on the second partial of the quintuplet on beat 3.

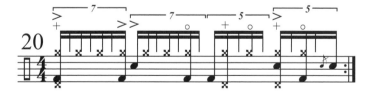

Once you're comfortable with these grooves, go back and create some of your own patterns using Exercises 5 through 8 as a framework. Exploring your own creativity is one of the most enjoyable aspects of learning new rhythms. The offbeat five-over-two hi-hat pattern from Exercise 7 is one of my favorite ways to phrase polyrhythms in a groove.

SECTION 6: A NEW PERSPECTIVE ON POLYRHYTHMS

This section of the book explores new ways to phrase polyrhythms with the base subdivision being doubled. This opens up a world of possibilities for orchestating polyrhythms in ways where none of the notes line up together.

Within the chapters, there are a number of different styles and frameworks being used. While only a handful of the rhythms are written out, be sure to pick the ones you like best and use them as a framework to explore each variation of the polyrhythm. This process takes time and dedication. But by working through each variation, you'll have a deep internalization of the polyrhythms, and you'll be able to start them from any point in the measure.

Make sure you practice each variation until it grooves and feels comfortable.

Enjoy the journey.

▶ PART 1: TWO OVER THREE

Typically, both sides of a polyrhythm begin together on the first note of the rhythm. We can vary this by displacing one or both sides of the rhythm. We'll focus on a two-over-three polyrhythm in 3/4. Dotted quarter notes comprise the two side of the rhythm, and quarter notes comprise the three side.

Exercise 1 displaces the two side by starting it on the "&" of beat 1. Notice that we still have two- and three-note groups of equally spaced notes within the same time frame.

The two side can be displaced by one more 8th note to start on beat 2. We can also displace the three side by an 8th note so it starts on the "&" of every beat.

Increasing the subdivision makes this concept especially interesting. If we double the subdivision from 8ths to 16ths we can create the same polyrhythm, but with the added option to create versions that have no point in which the two sides occur simultaneously. Exercise 2 demonstrates this concept by starting the two side on the "e" of beat 1 to create a linear polyrhythm.

I try to practice unique concepts like these within the context of a groove. This allows me to really feel how the rhythms work with or against the pulse, which is imperative if you want to apply what you're practicing musically. In the next few examples, we'll play 8th notes on the hi-hat, the two side of the polyrhythm on the snare, and the three side on the bass drum.

Exercises 3 and 4 demonstrate the two other positions for the two side in which it doesn't occur simultaneously with the three side.

Exercise 5 displaces the three side by a 16th note to the "e" of each beat.

Exercise 6 displaces both sides of the polyrhythm. For an interesting variation, try accenting the "&" of each beat on the hi-hat.

In Exercise 7, we're going to embellish the groove slightly. We'll start the two side on the "&" of beat 1 and our three side on the "a" of beat 1. There's also one additional bass drum note on beat 1. Accenting the "&" of each beat with the hi-hat adds an upbeat feel.

In the next example, we'll use the ride bell to represent our three side while playing the two side on the snare starting on the "a" of beat 1.

We can also take a *New Breed*–style approach by using the three side of this polyrhythm in an ostinato and leaving one limb free to play variations of the two side. In Exercise 9, the bass drum plays the three side on the "a" of each beat with an additional note on beat 1. With your right hand playing the ride cymbal and your left foot playing the "&" of each beat, your left hand is free to play each displacement of the two side. Here's the ostinato.

Here are the six placements of the two side of a two-over-three 16th-note polyrhythm.

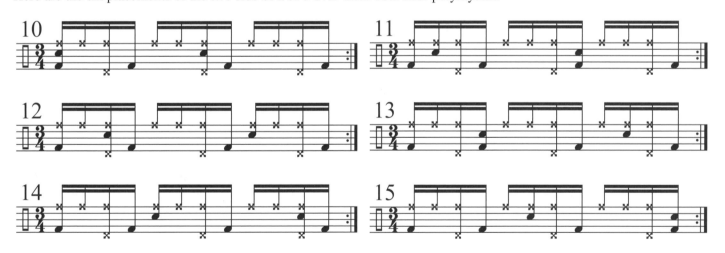

Next we'll apply the rhythm to a more challenging pattern. We'll use an ostinato that includes a snare on the "&" of beat 2 played with the right hand. The left hand plays the two side between a pair of bells or other small effects cymbals, as demonstrated in Exercises 16 and 17.

GOING BEYOND

We can also create unique variations with this polyrhythm by using 16th-note triplets. In 3/4, this subdivision contains eighteen 16th-note-triplet partials. The dotted quarter note is equivalent to nine 16th-note triplet partials, while the three side takes up six partials (which equals a quarter note). Exercise 18 places a basic two-over-three phrasing over a 16th-note-triplet double bass pattern. The three side is played on a china cymbal as quarter notes, and the two side is played on beat 1 and the "&" of beat 2.

Exercise 19 places the snare on the third partial of the 16th-note triplet on beat 2 and the last note of the 16th-note triplet on beat 4.

Also try displacing the three side within the 16th-note triplets. Exercise 20 moves the three side to the "&" of each beat while starting the two side on the second 16th-note triplet partial on beat 2.

As daunting as these examples may seem, always try to make them groove. Don't lose sight of musicality when diving into the polyrhythmic rabbit hole.

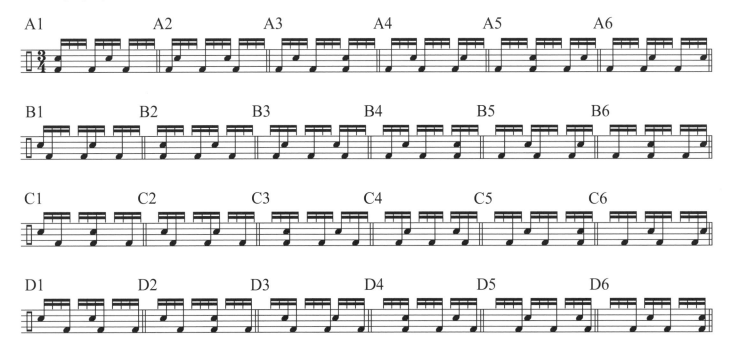

►PART 2: THREE OVER TWO

The three-over-two polyrhythm is made up of two contrasting rhythms (three equally spaced notes over two equally spaced notes) that are played simultaneously. We can build this polyrhythm by choosing one subdivision to act as a common denominator between the two rhythms. In this lesson, we'll use 8th-note triplets in 2/4. The quarter-note pulse comprises the "two" side, and every other triplet partial comprises the "three" side.

Within that 8th-note framework, we can displace either side (or both sides) of the polyrhythm to start on any part of the beat. The pattern starts to get especially interesting if you double the subdivision from 8th-note triplets to 16th-note triplets. Doing that allows you to displace the rhythm into positions where none of the notes line up at the same time, which results in a linear polyrhythm.

In Exercises 1–4, we'll displace the three side of the three-over-two polyrhythm to four positions within 16th-note triplets. Be sure to keep time with your left foot.

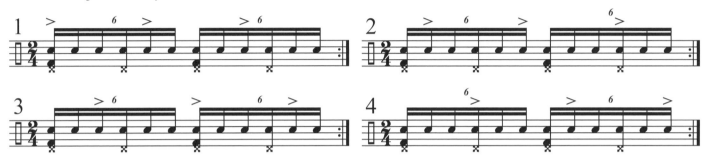

When you get the hang of the previous examples, it's time to start displacing the bass drum, which is outlining the two side of the polyrhythm. You can play the bass drum on any of the six partials of the 16th-note triplets. In Exercise 5, we're using the accents from Exercise 4 while moving the kick to the fourth partial of each 16th-note triplet.

Experiment with the six different kick positions under each of the accent patterns from Exercises 1-4. There's a total of twenty-four variations. When you can play the rhythms freely, try experimenting with a paradiddle sticking while moving the accents around the drumset.

One of my favorite ways to practice these rhythms is by using them as snare and bass drum comping figures under a swing ride pattern. Since the swing pattern is played in 8th-note triplets, the rhythm will take twice as long to complete within 4/4.

Let's use the swing context to explore some of the different bass drum variations. In Exercises 6–8, we'll keep the three side of the polyrhythm consistent on the snare while displacing the bass drum to different parts of the beat.

Once the three previous examples are comfortable, try the remaining placements as comping patterns. They're a lot of fun, and they'll help you internalize the rhythms on each part of the beat.

Next let's try something a bit heavier and put the 16th-note triplets on double bass. We'll voice the three side of the polyrhythm on the snare. We'll outline the two side using doubles within the kick pattern. This is a great workout for your feet. If you can't play left-foot doubles, simply reverse the patterns in Exercises 9 and 10 so that all of the doubled notes are played with the right foot.

In Exercise 9, the bass drum doubles start on the second partial of each 16th-note triplet while the three side of the polyrhythm starts on the third partial with the snare.

Exercise 10 places the double on the last partial of each beat while the snare starts the three side of the polyrhythm on the fourth partial of beat 1.

The last double bass variation we're going to try cuts the 8th-note ride pattern down to the "&" of each beat. The bass drum doubles are played on the fifth 16th-note-triplet partial, and the three side of the polyrhythm starts on the second partial with the snare.

The last feel we'll check out is a 16th-note-triplet shuffle. Play these examples on an auxiliary pair of hi-hats or the ride cymbal, because we'll be incorporating our hi-hat foot.

Exercise 12 starts both sides of the three-over-two polyrhythm on beat 1. The two side is played with the bass drum while the three side is played with the hi-hat foot. Take this slowly to work out the coordination.

Things start to get a little tricky in Exercise 13. The bass drum plays the two side on the third partial of each 16th-note triplet while also playing the downbeat. The hi-hat foot starts the three side of the polyrhythm on the second partial.

In Exercise 14, the hi-hat foot starts the three side of the polyrhythm on the third partial while the bass drum is placed on the last note of each 16th-note triplet.

The final shuffle example is challenging but fun. Each side of the polyrhythm starts on the second 16th-note-triplet partial. But opening and closing the hi-hat foot within the three side of the polyrhythm poses an interesting coordination challenge because the hi-hat foot splashes and shuts on unique parts of the beat. Learn the pattern without the openings at first, and keep the subdivision solid until you have the coordination down.

The best way to practice these rhythms is to pick one of the feels and work your way through every displacement of the polyrhythm. Then you can try to blend these rhythms into your own grooves.

►PART 3: THREE OVER FOUR

A three-over-four polyrhythm is comprised of sets of three equally spaced notes and four equally spaced notes that occupy the same timeframe. Typically both sides of the polyrhythm start together on the same note and utilize the same subdivision. If we look at a measure of 8th-note triplets in 4/4, we have a total of twelve notes that are divisible by both three and four. Quarter notes comprise the four side and will represent the pulse. The three side is created by playing every fourth triplet partial—**one**-trip-let, two-**trip**-let, three- trip-**let**, four-trip-let.

Exercise 1 demonstrates this with 8th-note triplets on the hi-hat and four quarter notes on the bass drum, while the three side of the polyrhythm is played on the snare.

Within an 8th-note-triplet framework, you can displace either one or both sides of the polyrhythm to start on any partial of the triplet. The rhythm starts to get especially interesting when you double the subdivision from 8th-note triplets to 16th-note triplets. Doing this allows you to displace one or both sides of the polyrhythm into positions where none of the notes from either side are played simultaneously.

Let's explore this using 16th-note triplets. There will be twice as many partials between each note of the four side of the polyrhythm. A great way to help internalize the spacing is by using a sticking pattern that fits evenly within it. There are eight 16th-note triplet partials between each beat of the three side, so let's assign a common sticking pattern—RLRR LRRL. The three side becomes clear when you accent the first note of the sticking.

Exercise 2 displaces the three side forward by one 16th-note-triplet partial. The sticking pattern is phrased between the snare and two pairs of hi-hats.

There are eight permutations of the three-note grouping in this polyrhythm. Experimenting with each position will help you internalize the feel of the three side from every point in the measure.

You can also displace the four side. Exercise 4 moves the four-note grouping to the "&" of the beat, with the left foot on the hi-hat, while the sticking pattern is voiced on the toms. Start by getting familiar with how the tom and snare pattern sounds against the left foot before adding the bass drum.

Exercise 5 voices the hand pattern between a pair of ride cymbals, with the left-hand accents placed on the bell.

In Exercises 6 and 7, the four side of the polyrhythm is played with quarter notes between the bass drum and snare, while an embellished ride cymbal pattern sits on top. The left foot is free to experiment with all eight permutations of the three side. In Exercise 6, the three-note grouping starts on the fourth 16th-note triplet partial, while in Exercise 7 it starts on the eighth. Make sure to start the rhythm on the six remaining partials as well.

While still playing the three side with the hi-hat foot, let's try a groove that accents the four side on the "&" of each beat with the ride bell. This time the three side starts on the fifth 16th-note triplet partial.

These rhythms get especially interesting when accenting the four side on less common partials. Exercises 9 and 10 have a syncopated right-hand pattern between the hi-hats and a stack. The stack accents the four side on the fifth 16th-note triplet partial. The kick and snare create a funky groove, and the three side is played with the left foot.

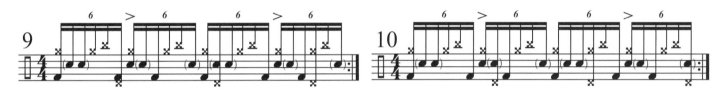

One of my favorite ways to play polyrhythms is within double bass grooves. In Exercise 11, the four side is voiced with bass drum doubles. The snare plays the three side starting on the third 16th-note-triplet partial.

In Exercise 12, both sides of the three-over-four polyrhythm start on the fifth 16th-note triplet partial of beat 1. We'll use the hi-hat and stack pattern from Exercises 9 and 10 to accent the four side of the polyrhythm.

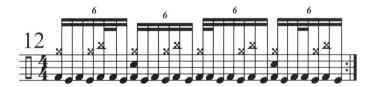

The next two examples use a similar double bass approach. However, this time we'll play alternating three-stroke ruffs instead of doubles. Exercise 13 applies this to the four side of the polyrhythm on the second 16th-note triplet partial. The three side is played with the snare starting on the downbeat.

Exercise 14 is an embellished groove that moves the three-stroke ruffs in the bass drum to the three side, starting on the second partial. The four side starts on the downbeat with quarter-note cymbal accents.

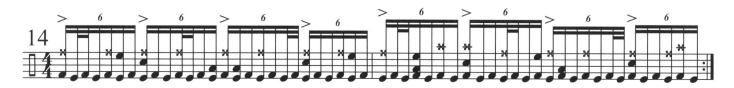

Exploring all eight of the three-note permutations and all six of the four-note permutations can be a lengthy process. We've only scratched the surface of what you can do with these ideas to expand your rhythmic palette. Be creative, and come up with your own ways to explore all of the possibilities as well.

▶ PART 4: FOUR OVER THREE

The four-over-three polyrhythm comprises four equally spaced notes and three equally spaced notes played simultaneously. We can build one by using a subdivision that both sides of the rhythm can fit within evenly. A measure of 16th notes in 3/4 gives us twelve notes that are evenly divisible by both four and three. By playing quarter notes, we get the three side of the polyrhythm. The four side is created by accenting every third 16th note.

Exercise 1 demonstrates a four-over-three polyrhythm applied to the bass drum and snare with a 16th-note hi-hat pattern that ties the rhythm together.

In the previous example, both sides of the polyrhythm start on the beat. Within a 16th-note framework, you can displace the four side to start on either the "e" or "&" of beat 1. If you start Exercise 1 on either beat 2 or beat 3, you'll see these permutations.

The possibilities get especially interesting when you displace the four side by one 32nd note, as notated in Exercise 2. Exercises 3 and 4 demonstrate the two remaining offbeat 32nd-note positions.

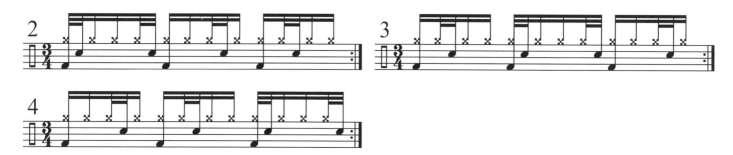

Practice these exercises slowly, count the 16th notes out loud, and focus on making the four side of the polyrhythm even. You're looking for the patterns to groove on autopilot until the four side of the polyrhythm feels evenly spaced. Keep your hi-hat and bass drum solid while running through all six variations.

When practicing advanced rhythmic concepts, developing them within a groove gives us a musical context. If you alternate between an ordinary 16th-note hi-hat beat and the exercises in this lesson, you can home in on how the pocket is supposed to feel. Make sure the polyrhythm remains consistent.

Next we'll incorporate a familiar ride pattern. Our hi-hat foot will play the "&" of each beat and represent the three side.

Practice exercises 5-7 by alternating each pattern with a straightforward groove, but maintain the notated hi-hat and ride cymbal pattern throughout both phrases. Try to maintain the same pulse from the basic groove when you play the polyrhythmic variations.

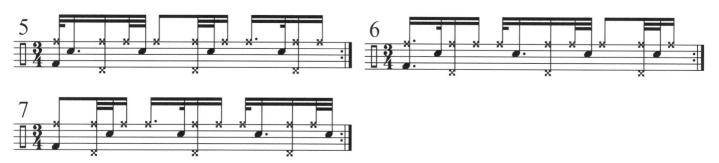

Once you've mastered Exercises 5–7, try accenting each snare note individually. For example, play Exercise 5 and ghost all the snare notes except the third. Do this for each snare note in the exercise, and come up with your own grooves that feature your favorite accents.

This next exercise adds a bass drum ostinato and moves the four side of the polyrhythm around the drumkit.

Next let's explore all of the possible permutations of this rhythm by playing a double bass pattern and splitting the four-over-three polyrhythm between our hands. In Exercise 9, the four side starts on the beat with our left hand on a rack tom. The three side, which so far has been represented by a quarter note on the bass drum or hi-hat foot, can also be displaced to any of the eight 32nd-note partials within each beat. We'll push the three side forward by one 32nd note with our right hand on a floor tom between the first and second bass drum notes of each beat.

Similar to how we accented each individual note of the four side in Exercises 5–7, try replacing each of the rack tom notes in Exercise 9 with the snare. In Exercise 10, the fourth rack tom note is played as a snare accent to create a syncopated groove. Be sure to practice these examples into and out of more standard 16th-note double bass grooves.

The next example pushes the four side forward by one 32nd note. The polyrhythm is now played entirely between the 16th-note double bass pattern. Go slowly, practice with a metronome, and make sure the rhythm sits evenly. Once comfortable, move each partial of the polyrhythm to an accented snare to isolate and solidify the feel of each note.

With your right hand between the first and second kick of each beat, experiment with the remaining permutations of the four side on the rack tom. Example 12 demonstrates one of these variations with the snare on beat 3.

Within this double bass framework, you can work your way through each permutation of both sides of the polyrhythm. The application of these rhythms and the context in which you practice them is only limited by your imagination. Exercise 13 demonstrates an offbeat variation that forms a tom melody between the bass drum pattern.

Now we'll voice the three side on the "e" of each beat and play four aggressive snare accents. Exercise 14 demonstrates a displaced feel when alternated with a more common 16th-note double bass groove. In Exercise 15 the snare pattern is pushed forward one 32nd note and lands entirely between the double bass pattern.

Come up with your own ways of voicing these rhythms musically while you work through the remaining variations. Think dynamically and musically while you explore these new rhythms to expand your own creativity.

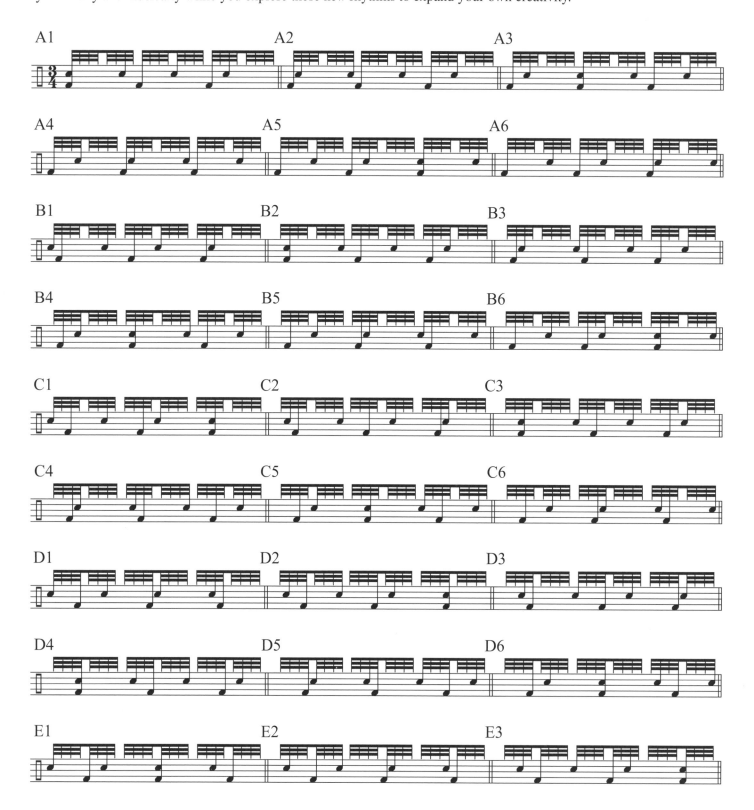

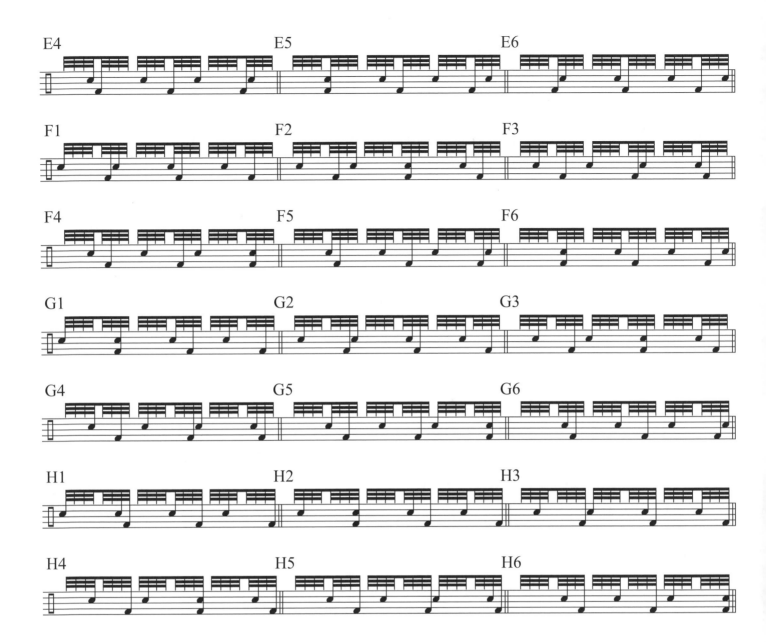

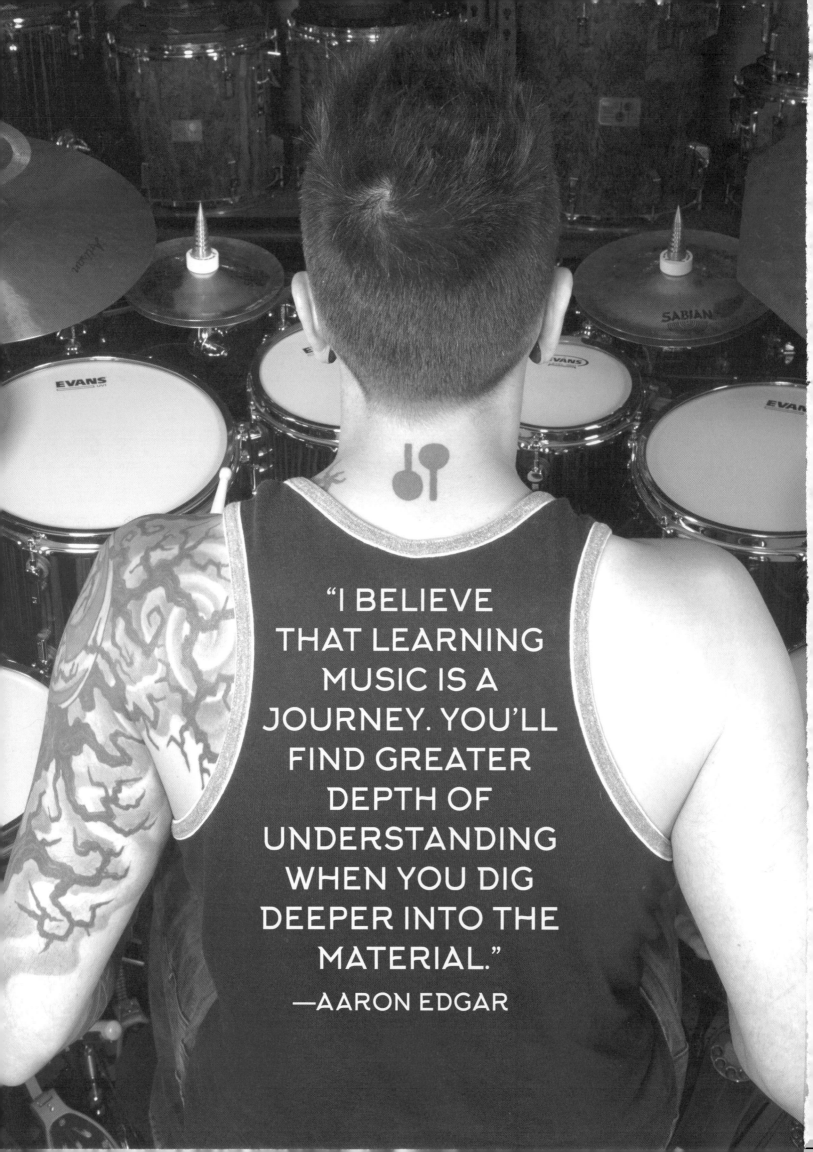

"I BELIEVE THAT LEARNING MUSIC IS A JOURNEY. YOU'LL FIND GREATER DEPTH OF UNDERSTANDING WHEN YOU DIG DEEPER INTO THE MATERIAL."

—AARON EDGAR